52

Write a poem a week.
Start now.
Keep going.

52

Write a poem a week.
Start now.
Keep going.

Jo Bell

with guest poets David Morley, Hilda Sheehan,
Kate Noakes, Matt Merritt, Luke Kennard,
Neil Rollinson, Angela France, Helen Mort,
Rachael Boast and Philip Gross.

Nine
Arches
Press

Jo Bell and guest poets
52: Write a Poem a Week. Start Now. Keep Going.

ISBN: 978-0-9931201-9-0

Design: 52 logo © David Gillett
http://davidgillett.co.uk

First published November 2015 by:

Nine Arches Press
PO Box 6269
Rugby
CV21 9NL
United Kingdom

www.ninearchespress.com

Printed in Britain by:
Imprint Digital

for Norman Hadley

About the Author

Jo Bell is a working poet. Erstwhile director of National Poetry Day and poet in residence at Glastonbury Festival, she runs poetry events and workshops across the UK. She teaches for the Poetry School, Arvon Foundation and Poetry Society. Her latest collection is *Kith*, published by Nine Arches Press in 2015.

Jo's online projects including *Bugged* and *52* use social networks and tight time constraints to build a sense of community, and to generate new poetry at a high standard. In 2015, the *52* project won a Saboteur Award and Jo Bell was awarded an honorary doctorate for services to poetry.

Follow @52Poetry on Twitter for news of more projects and for *52*-based events, including workshops and readings which bring this book to life.

Contents

RESOLUTION

This book comes with very simple instructions: *Write a poem a week. Start now. Keep going.* **You may be starting on 1st January or on midsummer's day, or on a wet Thursday in November; it doesn't matter. Start now. Try to keep writing for 52 weeks, a whole year – and then keep going.**

If you fall off the wagon, that also doesn't matter. Get back on, and keep writing for pleasure or, if you like, in hopes of publication and reputation. Of course, if you just want to dip in now and again, don't let me stop you; this book is a stimulus, a little kickstart for the Muse.

For me, 52 started one December evening. I had been a working poet for some years; writing my own work, teaching, mentoring, programming festivals and national projects, running online and face-to-face classes. I met many people who needed a little help to get writing, or to get back to writing. Yet many of the existing books or sites which offered writing prompts gave unfulfilling tasks – simple, two-dimensional things like 'Look at this box, what's inside it?' or formal challenges like 'write a sonnet about.....' as if any form could suit any subject. These sites treat the writer as a blank slate; they lead you down a narrow avenue of the prompter's making, rather than allowing you to explore your own experience from a new angle.

I knew, then, that there were many intelligent people who wrote poetry, or wanted to, but who didn't know how to get that little creative push that they needed. So I published a blog on New Year's Eve 2013/14 which read:

'Ready to take your writing seriously? Good. Then we'll begin. Every week, you get a new exercise to help you write a new poem. You write it your way – to the very best of your ability. You improve, you expand, you develop.

Watch this space. Begin this week – whichever week of the year it is. There will be guest writers supplying inspiration and ideas; poems to provoke, discuss and disgust; examples of the best poems from others in the 52 community.

Write hard, and clear, and well. One poem a week. Come on in.'

This was the beginning of the 52 project. In the following year I continued to supply one writing prompt a week, and invited ten big-name guest poets to contribute theirs. There was an online workshopping group, run by myself and fellow writer Norman Hadley, where people gathered to discuss the poems they had written in response to the prompts. All of this was free, and the group soon had hundreds of members. They became a lively ecology of poets, critics and friends, helping each other to improve and take risks in their work.

The rest is a small piece of poetry history. Poems written in response to these prompts have won or been shortlisted in international competitions and published in journals of high renown. MA and PhD courses have accepted students on the strength of them. New collections have been accepted by publishers on the basis of a portfolio of 52 poems. The project won a Saboteur award and an anthology, *The Very Best of 52* (edited by Jonathan Davidson, published by Nine Arches Press, 2015), was published.

That kind of success is rewarding and we all enjoyed it. But the real success is elsewhere, in the private conversation between poet and page which is encouraged by this book. If the prompts are sometimes forceful, that's because I'd like you to push yourself and write something worthwhile, something that you are proud of. Often we settle for the comfortable in poetry, and end up with trite poems that try to say too much, and say far too little. The process of writing, not the process of winning awards, is where the treasure is. As George Mitchell once said, 'The only thing you need to know about prizes is that Mozart never won one.'

Don't worry if your first efforts are not masterpieces; indeed, don't worry if you still feel that way after thirty years of writing. It's not just you. Be a little kind to yourself, and a little hard on yourself: if writing poetry is important to you, then try to give it some time. Every moment you spend on it is worthwhile but if you miss a week or two, that's fine. Life gets in the way; but since life is your raw material, you can't have too much of it.

I urge you, in particular, to read every one of the poems included in this book. They aren't there only for enjoyment, though they are certainly there for that. Each one illustrates something about technique or subject, and many are surprising. If there is one thing I want you to take from this book, it is this: *Nobody writes good poetry without reading good poetry.* Those who don't take this seriously invariably write clichéd, derivative and unoriginal work – just what we all want to avoid – because they aren't aware of the context in which they are writing.

We couldn't fit in all the poems we wanted to use without making this a building rather than a book, but where I mention a poem which isn't included in the book, it's possible to find it online – usually at the Poetry Foundation (poetryfoundation.org) or at the Poetry Archive (poetryarchive.org) by typing in the title. Both sites are full of gems and you may lose several hours, to your own advantage. Importantly, these sites reproduce poems accurately without typos or formatting mistakes, and with the consent of the poet or publisher. Many others will reproduce a copyright poem with lots of errors, and without permission or payment, so that both you and the poet are short-changed.

By all means use this book to teach your own class, so long as you acknowledge it as your source. I hope you'll find it refreshing. I hope you get some great poems out of it. I hope it changes your life a little. At the end of it, you may have written 52 new poems but more than that, you should see that you can write about anything. Anything.

Write a poem a week. Start now. Keep going.

Jo Bell,
November 2015.

1. EVERYTHING IS GOING TO BE AMAZING

Are you sitting comfortably? Never mind. Let's begin anyway. Welcome to 52, a weekly kick in the backside for your Muse. Here you will find prompts from big names and unexpected sources; starting points for poems, discussions and projects in your private writing life or to share with your poetry group.

What is poetry for? Everything. Every damn thing. Poetry can tell us how to live, question how we live, remind us how we choose to live.

The message of this book is simply: give yourself an hour a week to write, at least. And an hour a week to read others' poetry, *at least.* Take this seriously; poets can be divided into those who are interested in poetry, and those who are only interested in their own poetry. The latter are rarely worth reading themselves. The poems set out here for you to read are absolutely necessary to what I ask you to write.

This week our idea, our theme, our suggestion is – *how to approach a year.* Brace yourself and read this riotous piece overleaf.

LAUREN ZUNIGA

Everything is going to be amazing

Put on your knickers, girl. We gonna eat these heavy
decisions for breakfast. Smother 'em in gravy, wash 'em down
with Grown Ass Woman Soda.

We got this. This is the Big Girl Processing Plant.
Don't nobody work through their issues like we do. We swallow
abandonment and cough up independence.

You wanna scream? You see that freight train coming at you?
You havin' that lead-in-yo-legs dream again? Kick that
muthatruckin' train in its teeth and do a jig.

That's what you need. Some Mongolian Throat Singing action
and a can o' Riverdance. Unwad your drawers, Little Mama.
Let's go to the drag show.

Bust out yo corset, Sweet Ginger and show 'em all that bouillon.
We were made for the stomp. We were made out of spoon
whittlin' voodoo stew. Play those spoons, girl.

Don't let 'em take your dysfunction and turn it into a brothel.
That's YOUR dysfunction. You chop that shit up and make it
into a masterpiece. This is the year of Quit the Dumb Shit.

So, you know what that means?
Quit the dumb shit. Stop washing your pearls down
with swine. Get up off your Cadillac britches and show them motor

mouth badgers how it's done. Everything ain't gonna be alright.
Everything is going to be amazing.

You don't have to like this piece (or any other poem in this book) to see what it means, or the mood it conveys. So roll up your sleeves. Sit down and write in this spirit, about how you are going to tackle your year: not just your year of writing but your next whole year, whatever the date is today.

52 is NOT about writing half-assed workshop-standard poetry. Write the very best you can. Push yourself. Use your poetry to help you work out what you think about the world, or to express the truths you hold self-evident. Take risks. It's only paper, you know.

Turn over a new leaf and begin. Everything is going to be amazing.

2. TRAVELLING IN STYLE

Welcome to Week 2. If you've already fallen off the wagon, don't stress about it. No-one is going to jail you. Just get back on.

This weekly prompt is a short, sharp stimulus. Take it where you will. Be brave, not slavish. Ignore me when you like, but take the gist of the prompt and work with it. The balance between my imposed constraint and your freedom is where the good poetry is. Try to be your best self and write as deeply, as well as you can.

So, Week 2 of your writing year. Back to work – and for most of us work means making journeys by car, by train, on foot or bicycle or tram. Even the most mundane trip brings strong meat to the writer. Today, mine brought a blinding rainstorm, a sunlit flock of birds, a spent firework, a farm shop with the inexplicable sign LEARN TO DIVE HERE; and in between, a succession of roundabouts whose exits were all unfamiliar and colourless.

Journeys, short or long. Poems, short or long. You can do anything with your trip today.

So, make your usual journey today. Pay attention. Do not put the radio on in the car; do not take your phone on your walk. *Notice* things. Your poem might be about the journey, or an episode within it, or the bicycle you use to make it, or the man picking his nose in the next car, or the everyday possibility of a fatal crash, or the hole in your shoe, or the longing for a conversation on the bus that never happens.

Travel. Think. Write. Enjoy the ride.

MATT MERRITT

Desire Lines

'Do not go where the path may lead, go instead where there is no path and leave a trail.' – Ralph Waldo Emerson

Drought or drench draw them more clearly,
teach the secret geometry of hidden
or half-arsed purpose. For each

ribbon of rained-on intent,
tramped-down meander of resolve
that hardens into lane or jitty,

or even city street, another ten
remain as freehand scrawls, scribbles
at best, the chords and tangents

of long-forgotten arcs. A season's growth
softens edges, a work-crew and a one-off budget
tame the snake in the grass, or divide head

from tail, but a few days of scorching sun,
a week of winter, can reunite both
or sharpen the top-down perspective,

until each waste-ground's a history
of every passing idea and impulse, half-buried, half-
realised, but still being dreamed.

3. EXPOSING YOURSELF

Brace yourself – we're going to get naked this week.

Let's start with this fragment from Walt Whitman's long, long poem 'Song of Myself':

Through me forbidden voices,
Voices of sexes and lusts, voices veil'd and I remove the veil,
Voices indecent by me clarified and transfigur'd.

I do not press my fingers across my mouth,
I keep as delicate around the bowels as around the head and heart,
Copulation is no more rank to me than death is.

I believe in the flesh and the appetites,
Seeing, hearing, feeling, are miracles, and each part and tag of
    me is a miracle.

Divine am I inside and out, and I make holy whatever I touch
    or am touch'd from,
The scent of these arm-pits aroma finer than prayer,
This head more than churches, bibles, and all the creeds.

Now read Anna Swir's *Large Intestine*. For the next stage, you'll need a full length mirror and a room with a lock. Now – get your kit off. Look at yourself, slowly and solemnly. Don't just imagine it – *do* it. Your subject is **your own body**. If this unsettles you, stick with it. Have a go.

What are you – a beauty queen, a drag queen, a sexual being, an asthmatic or amputee, a person whose ordinary body is a vehicle for happiness or deceit? Your body is a means for fighting, fucking, fixing things. Shame it for letting you down.

Praise it for holding you together. Look at it as a new lover or old partner would; as a dog would; as a god would. Your scars, tattoos, hairline... it's all raw material.

Let me guess – your first instinct is to write a self-deprecating poem, a mildly amusing one in which you comment on your flawed or ageing body. Well, if you *want* to, then do it: no shame in that – Auden, for instance, addressed *A New Year's Greeting* to all the microbes in his body. But isn't that the easy way out? Perhaps you should dig deeper. Perhaps not. Your call.

This is unflinching stuff and requires every kind of self-exposure. It may not be comfortable. But then, you aren't here to be comfortable. You're here to write.

ANNA SWIR

Large Intestine

Look in the mirror. Let us both look.
Here is my naked body.
Apparently you like it,
I have no reason to.
Who bound us, me and my body?
Why must I die
together with it?
I have the right to know where the borderline
between us is drawn.
Where am I, I, I myself.

Belly, am I in the belly? In the intestines?
In the hollow of the sex? In a toe?
Apparently in the brain. I do not see it.
Take my brain out of my skull. I have the right
to see myself. Don't laugh.
That's macabre, you say.

It's not me who made
my body.
I wear the used rags of my family,
an alien brain, fruit of chance, hair
after my grandmother, the nose
glued together from a few dead noses.
What do I have in common with all that?
What do I have in common with you, who like
my knee, what is my knee to me?

Surely
I would have chosen a different model.

I will leave both of you here,
my knee and you.
Don't make a wry face, I will leave you all my body
to play with.
And I will go.
There is no place for me here,
in this blind darkness waiting for
corruption.
I will run out, I will race
away from myself.
I will look for myself
running
like crazy
till my last breath.

One must hurry
before death comes. For by then
like a dog jerked by its chain
I will have to return
into this stridently suffering body.
To go through the last
most strident ceremony of the body.

Defeated by the body,
slowly annihilated because of the body

I will become kidney failure
or the gangrene of the large intestine.
And I will expire in shame.

And the universe will expire with me,
reduced as it is
to a kidney failure
and the gangrene of the large intestine.

4. AN INVITATION

'Look here Vita — throw over your man, and we'll go to Hampton Court and dine on the river together and walk in the garden in the moonlight and come home late and have a bottle of wine and get tipsy, and I'll tell you all the things I have in my head, millions, myriads — They won't stir by day, only by dark on the river. Think of that. Throw over your man, I say, and come.'

I hope you feel welcoming; this week it's all about *writing an invitation.* The breathless one above is from Virginia Woolf to her lover Vita Sackville-West in 1926. Yours might likewise be addressed to a lover, or you could invite an old friend to dinner like the Elizabethan poet Ben Jonson *Inviting a Friend to Supper* or the Roman, Catullus in his invitation opposite.

Invite your teenage son to practice personal hygiene. Invite a corrupt president to step down, or a weak leader to step up. Write a breathless exhortation to take up cycling or masturbation. Invite your as-yet-unknown wife to show herself; invite the unconverted to faith, or to poetry. Ask a grandchild to a play-date, or an unborn child to come and share the world, or like Galway Kinnell here, ask a dead hero to join you.

Invite your long-standing partner to play Pooh Sticks at midnight in the nude. Ask the Muse to drop by your home, if you haven't seen her in a while. Invite the birds to dine on snails in your garden; invite Love or Courage to favour you at a time of need.

Whatever you write, your invitation must *offer something to entice* – fine wines, a damn good seeing-to, the best Pooh Sticks the Hundred Acre Wood can supply, the rewards of good conversation. Make it clear what you offer. Make the invitee feel that his or her company is essential to your happiness; be enticing, not merely courteous. Remember what *you* have to give.

You're issuing the invitation, not describing one or replying to one. Write your best, most welcoming, most irresistible poem of invitation. Throw over your family, your friends, everyone else I say, and come to the 52 party.

GAIUS VALERIUS CATULLUS

An Invitation to Fabullus

You'll dine well, in a few days, with me,
if the gods are kind to you, my dear Fabullus,
and if you bring lots of good food with you,
and don't come without a pretty girl
and wine and wit and all your laughter.
I say you'll dine well, and charmingly,
if you bring all that: since your Catullus's
purse alas is full of cobwebs.
But accept endearments in return for the wine
or whatever's sweeter and finer:
since I'll give you a perfume my girl
was given by the Loves and Cupids,
and when you've smelt it, you'll ask the gods
to make you, Fabullus, all nose.

Oatmeal

I eat oatmeal for breakfast.
I make it on the hot plate and put skimmed milk on it.
I eat it alone.
I am aware it is not good to eat oatmeal alone.
Its consistency is such that it is better for your mental health if
    somebody eats it with you.
That is why I often think up an imaginary companion to have
    breakfast with.
Possibly it is even worse to eat oatmeal with an imaginary
    companion.
Nevertheless, yesterday morning I ate my oatmeal with John Keats.
Keats said I was right to invite him: due to its glutinous texture,
gluey lumpishness, hint of slime, and unusual willingness to
disintegrate, oatmeal must never be eaten alone.
He said it is perfectly OK, however, to eat it with an imaginary
    companion,
and he himself had enjoyed memorable porridges with Edmund
    Spenser and John Milton.
He also told me about writing the "Ode to a Nightingale."
He wrote it quickly, he said, on scraps of paper, which he then
    stuck in his pocket,
but when he got home he couldn't figure out the order of the
    stanzas, and he and a friend spread the papers on a table, and
    they made some sense of them, but he isn't sure to this day if
    they got it right.
He still wonders about the occasional sense of drift between stanzas,
    and the way here and there a line will go into the configuration
    of a Moslem at prayer, then raise itself up and peer about, then
    lay itself down slightly off the mark, causing the poem to move
    forward with God's reckless wobble.

He said someone told him that later in life Wordsworth heard
about the scraps of paper on the table, and tried shuffling some
stanzas of his own, but only made matters worse.
When breakfast was over, John recited "To Autumn."
He recited it slowly, with much feeling, and he articulated the
words lovingly, and his odd accent sounded sweet.
He didn't offer the story of writing "To Autumn," I doubt if there
is much of one.
But he did say the sight of a just-harvested oat field got him started
on it and two of the lines, "For Summer has o'er-brimmed their
clammy cells" and "Thou watchest the last oozings hours by
hours," came to him while eating oatmeal alone.
I can see him – drawing a spoon through the stuff, gazing into the
glimmering furrows, muttering – and it occurs to me:
maybe there is no sublime, only the shining of the amnion's tatters.
For supper tonight I am going to have a baked potato left over
from lunch.
I'm aware that a leftover baked potato can be damp, slippery, and
simultaneously gummy and crumbly,
and therefore I'm going to invite Patrick Kavanagh to join me.

5. THE MASTERY OF THE THING

Our first guest poet is the prolific, innovative and much-lauded Professor David Morley. David's own poetry draws on his Romani heritage, his reading of John Clare and other poetic predecessors – and, in this case, his deep love for birds. He writes:

This week, both you and your poem will leap off a cliff. You will not fall, gall yourself, and gash gold-vermilion. You will soar.

Ted Hughes urged us in *The Making of a Poem* to: 'Imagine what you are writing about. See it and live it. Do not think it up laboriously, as if you were working out mental arithmetic. Just look at it, touch it, smell it, listen to it, turn yourself to it. When you do this, the words look after themselves, like magic.'

That is how you are going to write this week's poem. It will feel as natural as breathing.

Practise hovering first. Please *speak aloud* Gerard Manley Hopkins' 'The Windhover', opposite. As the naturalist Chris Packham said in a recent short film of kestrels, 'by constantly making small adjustments to their wings and tail feathers these kestrels can keep their head and their large eyes completely steady'. Try this as you begin to write your poem.

Choose an animal. Observe it as closely as possible in the wild or a zoo or aviary. Then become it. See it and live it. Look at it, touch it, smell it, listen to it, turn yourself to it. Hopkins inhabits the living bird; he lets the movement buckle and brace his word-choice. The poem emerges from a kestrel's physicality into which Hopkins has leapt – through an action (almost an inaction) of what John Keats called *negative capability.*

The novelist A.L. Kennedy and I once held a writing workshop to which we invited a Gyrfalcon, a Scops Owl, two Harrier Hawks and a Barn Owl. Alison later remarked how 'the writer's and the raptor's eye are – like the poet's and the lover's eyes – intimately related and it is valuable for us to consider them.' Consider this: what is it really like to fly? Become that falcon.

AND the fire that breaks from thee then, a billion Times told lovelier, more dangerous, O my chevalier!

And the words will look after themselves. Like magic. And your heart will no longer be in hiding.

GERARD MANLEY HOPKINS

The Windhover

To Christ our Lord

I caught this morning morning's minion, king-
    dom of daylight's dauphin, dapple-dawn-drawn Falcon,
        in his riding
Of the rolling level underneath him steady air, and striding
High there, how he rung upon the rein of a wimpling wing
In his ecstasy! then off, off forth on swing,
    As a skate's heel sweeps smooth on a bow-bend: the hurl
        and gliding
    Rebuffed the big wind. My heart in hiding
Stirred for a bird, – the achieve of, the mastery of the thing!

Brute beauty and valour and act, oh, air, pride, plume, here
   Buckle! AND the fire that breaks from thee then, a billion
Times told lovelier, more dangerous, O my chevalier!

   No wonder of it: shéer plód makes plough down sillion
Shine, and blue-bleak embers, ah my dear,
   Fall, gall themselves, and gash gold-vermilion.

6. SKY WRITING

Weather. There is a lot of it about. But as a subject, weather is *dull*, as everybody knows.

Really? Tell that to Ted Hughes. Read his poem 'Wind' overleaf. Just look at those verbs – *crashing, booming, stampeding, floundering, flexing, blinding, dented, drummed.* They're in your face – you hear and feel them. The verb is the engine of a poem, giving a sense of movement or mood (are you walking across a room or skipping, sashaying, slouching?). In this one verbs really pull their weight, lending the poem energy.

I once tried to write about a bad relationship, and failed. I gave up and wrote instead about the snow that day. I wrote how it masked the landscape and silenced everything – bleak, cold, malevolent. And lo – a poem about a bad relationship. In another mood I might have written about snow's brightness, its purity, the children sledging. A poem is never actually about what it's about. You can write about the same thing on two different days, and get entirely different results.

So: **write about the weather.** But make it more than polite conversation. *Describe* it – how it feels on the end of your nose or the roof of your car; how it sounds against the window; how it changes the landscape or throws shadows inside. Flood and drought, fallen trees and sun-dappled fields. See at the end if you really *have* written about weather.

Or start with remembered weather. That day of kite-flying on the beach; the time you got lost on a misty fell; a snowball fight, an afternoon of sunny love-making. Don't be predictable. Allow yourself to gag for rain, like the Tudor lover in our loneliest English poem or rage against the sun, as John Donne did in the best ever love poem, both following Hughes' poem here. You can only see the world, the weather, the furniture, through your mood today. Take your time, think your way around it, find a way in but don't try too hard. Weather, like death and taxes, is always with us.

Tell us about it. Make the grey skies fizz. Make the blue skies sing.

TED HUGHES

Wind

This house has been far out at sea all night,
The woods crashing through darkness, the booming hills,
Winds stampeding the fields under the window
Floundering black astride and blinding wet

Till day rose; then under an orange sky
The hills had new places, and wind wielded
Blade-light, luminous black and emerald,
Flexing like the lens of a mad eye.

At noon I scaled along the house-side as far as
The coal-house door. Once I looked up –
Through the brunt wind that dented the balls of my eyes
The tent of the hills drummed and strained its guyrope,

The fields quivering, the skyline a grimace,
At any second to bang and vanish with a flap:
The wind flung a magpie away and a black-
Back gull bent like an iron bar slowly. The house

Rang like some fine green goblet in the note
That any second would shatter it. Now deep
In chairs, in front of the great fire, we grip
Our hearts and cannot entertain book, thought,

Or each other. We watch the fire blazing,
And feel the roots of the house move, but sit on,
Seeing the window tremble to come in,
Hearing the stones cry out under the horizons.

ANON

Westron Wind

Oh western wind, when wilt thou blow
that the small rain down can rain?
Christ, if my love were in my arms
and I in my bed again!

JOHN DONNE

The Sunne Rising

Busy old fool, unruly sun,
      Why dost thou thus,
Through windows, and through curtains call on us?
Must to thy motions lovers' seasons run?
      Saucy pedantic wretch, go chide
      Late school boys and sour prentices,
    Go tell court huntsmen that the king will ride,
    Call country ants to harvest offices,
Love, all alike, no season knows nor clime,
Nor hours, days, months, which are the rags of time.

      Thy beams, so reverend and strong
      Why shouldst thou think?
I could eclipse and cloud them with a wink,
But that I would not lose her sight so long;
      If her eyes have not blinded thine,
      Look, and tomorrow late, tell me,
    Whether both th' Indias of spice and mine
    Be where thou leftst them, or lie here with me.
Ask for those kings whom thou saw'st yesterday,
And thou shalt hear, All here in one bed lay.

      She's all states, and all princes, I,
      Nothing else is.
Princes do but play us; compared to this,
All honor's mimic, all wealth alchemy.
      Thou, sun, art half as happy as we,
      In that the world's contracted thus.
    Thine age asks ease, and since thy duties be
    To warm the world, that's done in warming us.
Shine here to us, and thou art everywhere;
This bed thy center is, these walls, thy sphere.

7. THIS SPORTING LIFE

Sport. Personally I hate it. Yes, all of it. The Winter Olympics, the Summer Olympics, the village egg-and-spoon race. But if humans do it, then poets can write about it. Poetry doesn't always have to be about the things we like; and as the poems that follow will show, a poem can go far beyond its apparent subject.

A poem, then, *about sport.* If you can write from direct experience then do so – speak as a marathon runner, a five-a-side player, a member of the girls' hockey team. Get specific, get physical. Be precise about the sensation of swimming, fast as a shark; the smells and colours of sport; the day you tried golf because you fancied the club professional. Perhaps your pastime, like Norman MacCaig's 'Fishing the Balvaig' overleaf, is more private.

Does the rhythm of your sport give you a ready-made shape, a refrain – the half-time break, the matches and sets, the stages of the race? Balance your language carefully – enough sporting language to show that you know the game, but not so much as to befuddle or annoy. If you need a refresher, read the back pages of the newspaper to borrow some classic sport-speak.

Spectators have voices too. Stand on the terraces with your tribe chanting COME ON YOU BLUES like George Szirtes in the following poem. Revisit your favourite sporting events on YouTube to remind you of the moment. Cheer from the sofa as the Grand National finishes; make the cricketers' tea; glimpse golfers on the hillside as you look up from the bus stop. I once pulled up in my narrowboat outside the pub where a hundred people were watching Andy Murray win Wimbledon – a memorable sporting moment, but one I remember because I was doing something else. Be physical, and tell us what *your* body is doing as you watch, how the blood is racing or the flu setting in.

Alternatively, go off-piste and start from a sporting fixture, but take a tangent. Be tragic, silly, polemical. The phrase 'China is the dominant force in table tennis' might catch your ear on the radio, or you may recall Monica Seles being stabbed on court. Start an imaginary affair with a sports commentator and describe his commentary in bed. Start, as always, from true observation. But, as always, take us further.

Play up! Play up! And play the game. 52, not out.

NORMAN MacCAIG

Fishing the Balvaig

It is like being divided, stood on stumps
On a layer of water scarcely thicker than light
That parallels away to show it's water all right.

While underneath two sawn-off waders walk
Surprisingly to one's wishes – as though no man
Moved lumpishly, so, but a sort of Caliban.

The eel that tries to screw his ignorant head
Under an instep thinks the same; and goes
Like a tape of water going where the water flows.

Collecting images by redounding them
The stream is leafed, sunned skied and full of shade;
Pot-holed with beer and shallowed with lemonade.

But in the glides is this thicker sort of light.
It blurs no freckled pebble or nervous weed,
Whose colours quicken as it slacks the speed.

As though water and light were mistranslations of
A vivifying influence they both use
To make a thing more thing and old news, news.

Which all the world is, wheeling round this odd
Divided figure, who forgets to pass
Through water that looks like the word isinglass.

GEORGE SZIRTES

Preston North End

Tottenham Hotspur versus Preston North End.
Finney's last season: my first. And my dad
with me. How surprisingly well we blend

with these others. Then the English had
the advantage, but today we feel
their fury, sadness and pity. There were some bad

years in between, a lot of down-at-heel
meandering. For me though, the deep blue
of Preston was ravishment of a more genteel,

poetic kind. They were thrashed five-one, it's true,
and Finney was crocked by Mackay. Preston went down,
hardly to rise again. But something got through

about Finney the plumber, Lancashire, the Crown,
and those new days a-coming. The crowd dissolves,
but we are of the crowd, heading into town

under sodium street lights. This year Wolves
will win the title. Then Burnley. I will see
Charlton, Law and George Best. The world revolves

around them and those voices on TV
reading the results. I'm being bedded in –
to what kind of soil remains a mystery,

but I sense it in my marrow like a thin
drift of salt blown off the strand. I am
an Englishman, wanting England to win.

I pass the Tebbitt test. I am Alan Lamb,
Greg Rusedski, Viv Anderson, the boy
from the corner shop, Solskjaer and Jaap Stam.

I feel no sense of distance when the tannoy
plays Jerusalem, Rule Britannia or the National Anthem.
I know King Priam. I have lived in Troy.

8. HIGH SOCIETY

Been to the corner shop lately? Have a look at Daljit Nagra's lively poem of shop life, 'Singh Song!', overleaf.

Now, consider the rich, untold stories of **your high street.** Every shop front holds human interest, including the empty ones. The optician where someone has just been told she is going blind; the library where Big Kev goes every day to secretly read romantic novels; the newsagent whose wife is climbing Everest as he serves you. Charity shops full of dead men's shoes; the market, with its con men and hearty traders. Everything we do in life is charged – even ordering a coffee may bring a string of associations. Follow that string. Who *was* WH Smith anyway?

For every prompt, there's a pitfall. This week, don't just illustrate. Make this more than a Lowry painting full of detail – more than a list of shops, more than an oh-where-are-they-now lament for the days of the butcher, the baker, the candlestick maker. Celebrate the cornucopian delights of Aldi, the confessional privacy of the hairdresser. Be a child, a dog, a pigeon. Make it rich, vivid with detail and randomness. Revisit Dylan Thomas' *Under Milk Wood* to see how a genius paints his town.

A suggestion: try not to include yourself in this one at all – no 'I', no 'me'. Above all, beware the boring poem, the poem which is only a snapshot of a place. Why not make the street a setting for a fight or a visitation from the Angel Gabriel? Include a snippet of overheard speech. Think about its atmosphere at dawn, at midnight.

Look up from the shop fronts to see their architecture and history – the Ship Inn, now a place where ladettes get wrecked on a Friday. Notice details; the medieval market cross, the coat of arms over that alleyway, the names of back lanes, a public sculpture with a cone on its head. Look as closely as Tony Hoagland does at 'The Galleria Shopping Mall' – at Starbucks, full of mums and toddlers – at the Indian greengrocer, full of bright vegetables and sari-clad shoppers.

Surprise yourself. Experiment with form and sound. Go to town.

DALJIT NAGRA

Singh Song!

i run just one ov my daddy's shops
from 9 o'clock to 9 o'clock
and he vunt me not to hav a break
but ven nobody in, i do di lock —

cos up di stairs is my newly bride
vee share in chapatti
vee share in di chutney
after vee hav made luv
like vee rowing through Putney —

ven i return vid my pinnie untied
di shoppers always point and cry:
hey Singh, ver yoo bin?
yor lemons are limes

yor bananas are plantain
dis dirty little floor need a little bit of mop
in di worst Indian shop
on di whole Indian road —

above my head high heels tap di ground
as my vife on di net is playing wid di mouse
ven she catch di cat she couple up a pair
book dem for a date on her lover's web page —

my bride,
she effing at my mum
in all di colours of Punjabi
my bride,
she stumble like a drunk
making fun at my daddy
my bride,
tiny eyes ov a gun
and di tummy ov a teddy
my bride,
she hav a red crew cut
and she wear a Tartan sari
a donkey jacket and some pumps
on di squeak ov di girls who are buy my penny sweeties —

Ven i return from di tickle ov my bride
di shoppers always point and cry:
hey Singh, ver yoo bin?
di milk is out ov date
and di bread is alvays stale
the tings yoo hav on offer yoo hav never got in stock
in di worst Indian shop
on di whole Indian road —

late in di midnight hour
ven yoo shoppers are wrap up quiet
ven di precinct is concrete-cool
vee cum down whispering stairs
and sit on my silver stool
from behind di chocolate bars
vee stare past di half-price window signs
at di beaches ov di UK in di brightey moon —

from di stool each night she say,
how much do yoo charge for dat moon baby?
from di stool each night i say,
is half di cost ov yoo baby.
from di stool each night she say,
how much does dat come to baby?
from di stool each night i say,
is priceless baby —

TONY HOAGLAND

At the Galleria Shopping Mall

Just past the bin of pastel baby socks and underwear,
there are some 49-dollar Chinese-made TVs;

one of them singing news about a far-off war,
one comparing the breast size of an actress from Hollywood

to the breast size of an actress from Bollywood.
And here is my niece Lucinda,

who is nine and a true daughter of Texas,
who has developed the flounce of a pedigreed blonde

and declares that her favorite sport is shopping.
Today is the day she embarks upon her journey,

swinging a credit card like a scythe
through the meadows of golden merchandise.

Today is the day she stops looking at faces,
and starts assessing the labels of purses;

So let it begin. Let her be dipped in the dazzling bounty
and raised and wrung out again and again.

And let us watch.
As the gods in olden stories

turned mortals into laurel trees and crows
            to teach them some kind of lesson,

so we were turned into Americans
to learn something about loneliness.

9. EVERYTHING IS CHANGED

Our second guest prompt is by Hilda Sheehan. Surreal, funny and/or disturbing, her poems can be found in her first collection *The Night My Sister Went to Hollywood*. Her work in poetry development has been recognised with a Poetry Can award. Hilda writes:

When I read a 'great' poem, there's a powerful psychological and physical reaction that happens, and I feel changed by it. Some years back I decided to read the *Norton Anthology of Poetry* from beginning to end, which was thrilling, until I reached Kenneth Koch ... and I stopped. I bought his books, and I read him until I couldn't read another poem by any other poet. I did of course. I found Mina Loy, Wallace Stevens...

In his *Art of Poetry*, Koch asks of our poems, 'Is it astonishing?' Now that's a big ask. How do we write astonishing poems? Do we always have to? And what makes them so? Sometimes it's a quiet poem, one that opens up new possibilities, like Robert Vas Dias' prose poem 'Do Angels Eat?' which you can find at robertvasdias.com. Or something sad, strange and funny like Rhoda Janzen's 'Raz El Hanout', which you'll find opposite.

Many really surprising poems like this include a transformation, large or small – so can you write *a story of change*? How did you feel at the beginning and what changes occurred? Don't necessarily create a poem at this stage: 'free write', jotting down whatever comes into your head. What amazing sounds can you pack in? What tone are you aiming for? Play with the syntax, break out of making perfect sense, go wild, be very naughty!

What can some Raz El Hanout do when rubbed into the lines of your poems?

RHODA JANZEN

Raz el Hanout

A recipe for lamb tagine
demands a mysterious
ingredient: raz el hanout.
Animal, vegetable, compound

of kings like myrrh? I decide
not to look it up, to wait and
see. At first it is everything
we seek but can't express.

Then it reverses: everything
thrust upon us—think fast!—
by the universe, like the leg
my friend Tom caught when

a cyclist got clipped by a car,
the driver stinking drunk
at 9:00 AM. Severed above
the knee, the leg flung itself

into the air, a javelin. Tom,
always quick, reached up and
caught it. But the story has
a twist. After the cyclist died

in an ambulance, the widow
inexplicably came on to Tom.
Not that Tom is unattractive.
Indeed he is the sort of man

I'd throw myself at if I were
a leg. It's hard to imagine
the sex that Tom and this
woman would have had

there in the hotel room
with the blackout curtains
pulled. I've never had sex
with Tom myself, but if I had

been that leg or that woman
I might have whispered,
"What fine reflexes you
have, Sir!" "Sir, say something

tender!" "Cradle me against
the guttural gasp from your
solar plexus." "Oh, Sir, I
sense the tip of bone

on skin, a surge of déjà vu."
"I am coming, I am about
to come, your shuddering
lover, your raz el hanout."

10. TOUCHED

your pal ruffled ma hat
i said, what? made the mistake of leaning forward
and that was that

blood-metal darkness and the taste of brass
the bell was rung
i know i went somewhere
because i had to come back.

It's not always pleasant to come into contact with someone else, as William Letford's poem 'Taking a Headbutt' shows. *Touch* is our subject for this week.

Touch can be ritualised, as in Mass; and a very simple and strong blessing it can be. It can be the touch of something against your skin, as in the Kim Addonizio poem which follows. Or it might be unsettling. Do you remember the first time you touched... one of *those*?

Often the sensation of touch is unremarked. When you put on a scratchy jumper, shake hands with a car dealer, hold hands with a lover – when you wash your face or a grandchild's hair, stuff a chicken or scratch an itch, get your prostate poked by the doctor – it's all touch. The sensation of your partner sleeping against you, or the loss of that sensation. The hairdresser's gentle massage; jostling someone on the bus.

Don't look too hard for your subject. It might be touch between humans, but it could be scrubbing potatoes or gardening. It could be a third-party example, observed. Just *pay attention* to a real instance of touch; the temperature, the sensation of grit or winceyette.

If the story turns out to be larger, then follow it. Ask yourself what you're really remembering. Why do you remember that handshake so well – because it was fake, or because it was a formal exchange when you actually wanted to kiss?

When you're done, examine the first few lines. Does the reader need those, or are they just an indulgent introduction? Look at the last few lines – are you telling the reader what you mean? Don't – you should have done that already by the choice of incident, setting, verbs. Take out *every* lazy abstract – love, grief, passion. Don't hand it to us on a plate; do your work as a poet, and show us.

Touch us, in fact.

KIM ADDONIZIO

"What Do Women Want?"

I want a red dress.
I want it flimsy and cheap,
I want it too tight, I want to wear it
until someone tears it off me.
I want it sleeveless and backless,
this dress, so no one has to guess
what's underneath. I want to walk down
the street past Thrifty's and the hardware store
with all those keys glittering in the window,
past Mr. and Mrs. Wong selling day-old
donuts in their café, past the Guerra brothers
slinging pigs from the truck and onto the dolly,

hoisting the slick snouts over their shoulders.
I want to walk like I'm the only
woman on earth and I can have my pick.
I want that red dress bad.
I want it to confirm
your worst fears about me,
to show you how little I care about you
or anything except what
I want. When I find it, I'll pull that garment
from its hanger like I'm choosing a body
to carry me into this world, through
the birth-cries and the love-cries too,
and I'll wear it like bones, like skin,
it'll be the goddamned
dress they bury me in.

11. SONGS OF PRAISE

Brothers and sisters, raise your hands – and raise your voice in praise.

Praise is one of the oldest traditions in poetry. The oldest epics celebrate a hero, a god; the patient wife or sexy queen, the bold warrior or wily hunter. Since then we've had praise for God, for plums, and the famous poem opposite by Christopher Smart, writing about his cat from an eighteenth-century asylum. Also following is Kathleen Jamie's poem of praise for pretty much everything in a flawed world.

Praise, then. Put someone on a pedestal: honour the praised, at the expense of the praiser.

You might choose an individual, but a parent or partner will be very hard to write about without mawkishness. A little distance could be useful. Celebrate a friend, a hero, a stranger. Sing out their story, their virtues. Concentrate on one episode if you can. Rosa Parks' trembling hand as she takes her seat in the whites-only area of the bus; the trapeze artist's strong arm; the painter's eye for colour; the drag artist shimmying onto stage.

Or choose something wider – a phenomenon, a class of people, an institution. Write In Praise of Clouds, Climbers, Coincidence or the Perfectly Ripe Pear of Wild Swimmers, Feminism, The Opposable Thumb.

Let your title lift weight out of the poem, so that you don't spend the first three lines explaining what your subject is. Perhaps write in the third person – not 'you did this lovely thing' but 'James did this lovely thing' or 'Blessed be the Cheesemakers, for they....' Above all, resist those abstracts – *grace, courage, love*. They may underlie what you want to say, but these words can seriously over-rev the engine of a poem.

This one isn't about you. Step back into the wings and let another take centre stage. Be silly, be funny or deathly serious but applaud the thing you admire with gusto. The reader should walk away from this poem uplifted, and looking at its subject with fresh respect.

Praise is more than like. It's a deep acclamation, a celebration of style or substance. Find the best of yourself in praising something else. Lift your voice, and raise the roof.

CHRISTOPHER (KIT) SMART

from Jubilate Agno

For I will consider my Cat Jeoffry.
For he is the servant of the Living God duly and daily
    serving him.
For at the first glance of the glory of God in the East he
    worships in his way.
For this is done by wreathing his body seven times round
with elegant quickness.
For then he leaps up to catch the musk, which is the blessing
    of God upon his prayer.
For he rolls upon prank to work it in.
For having done duty and received blessing he begins to
    consider himself.
For this he performs in ten degrees.

For first he looks upon his forepaws to see if they are clean.

For secondly he kicks up behind to clear away there.

For thirdly he works it upon stretch with the forepaws extended.

For fourthly he sharpens his paws by wood.

For fifthly he washes himself.

For sixthly he rolls upon wash.

For seventhly he fleas himself, that he may not be interrupted upon the beat.

For eighthly he rubs himself against a post.

For ninthly he looks up for his instructions.

For tenthly he goes in quest of food.

For having consider'd God and himself he will consider his neighbour.

For if he meets another cat he will kiss her in kindness.

For when he takes his prey he plays with it to give it a chance.

For one mouse in seven escapes by his dallying.

For when his day's work is done his business more properly begins.

For he keeps the Lord's watch in the night against the adversary.

For he counteracts the powers of darkness by his electrical skin and glaring eyes.

For he counteracts the Devil, who is death, by brisking about the life.

For in his morning orisons he loves the sun and the sun loves him.

For he is of the tribe of Tiger.

KATHLEEN JAMIE

The Way We Live

Pass the tambourine, let me bash out praises
to the Lord God of movement, to Absolute
non-friction, flight, and the scarey side:
death by avalanche, birth by failed contraception.
Of chicken tandoori and reggae, loud, from tenements,
commitment, driving fast and unswerving
friendship. Of tee-shirts on pulleys, giros and Bombay,
barmen, dreaming waitresses with many fake-gold
bangles. Of airports, impulse, and waking to uncertainty,
to strip-lights, motorways, or that pantheon —
the mountains. To overdrafts and grafting

and the fit slow pulse of wipers as you're
creeping over Rannoch, while the God of moorland
walks abroad with his entourage of freezing fog,
his bodyguard of snow.
Of endless gloaming in the North, of Asiatic swelter,
to launderettes, anecdotes, passions and exhaustion,
Final Demands and dead men, the skeletal grip
of government. To misery and elation; mixed,
the sod and caprice of landlords.
To the way it fits, the way it is, the way it seems
to be: let me bash out praises – pass the tambourine.

12. THE SKY AT NIGHT

'When we contemplate the whole globe as one great
dewdrop, striped and dotted with continents and
islands, flying through space with all the other stars, all
singing and shining together as one, the whole universe
appears as an infinite storm of beauty.' – John Muir

You're a poet, right? Staring at the sky and thinking great
thoughts is basically your job. So, get some stars in your
eyes. Look up to *the sky at night* and the many interesting
sparkly objects therein.

Go outside tonight, and take some quiet time to just
look. Comets, the moon, the planets, the International Space
Station and the people working in it, the Northern Lights;
and beyond the visible, the millions of unseen galaxies.
Who is up there right now, looking down at us in wonder
– or pooing in a plastic bag? Remember glimpsing the Hale-
Bopp comet over the garage in 1997; the shine of different
constellations over Africa or the Outback; the night you
were disappointed by a lunar eclipse.

There is a grand magic here, if you handle it
carefully. There is also a vast universe full of cliché, and
swirly mists of cosmic piffle. How to avoid it? With humour,
like Billy Collins opposite. Or find Robert Frost's long poem
'The Star-Splitter' online to see big themes lightly handled.
These poems aren't about stars at all. They only *start* from
stars.

Consider your astrological sign (but don't go all tie-dye on
us). Explore stellar stories – not just the star of Bethlehem,
but look up the myths behind Cassiopeia or Orion. Seek
out individual stars, their names and legends, or the images

of space taken by the Hubble telescope.

If you go out and see nothing but clouds, or you get cold and give up – that's a poem too. In poetry, we can make bricks without straw. After all, David Constantine didn't see dolphins, but from the experience of looking for them he got the poem overleaf. It has nothing to do with space, but I make no apology for that. Yours may likewise turn out to be about longing, or searching, or the experience of giving up.

Look up. Get some space. Cosmic.

BILLY COLLINS

Man in Space

All you have to do is listen to the way a man
sometimes talks to his wife at a table of people
and notice how intent he is on making his point
even though her lower lip is beginning to quiver,

and you will know why the women in science
fiction movies who inhabit a planet of their own
are not pictured making a salad or reading a magazine
when the men from earth arrive in their rocket,

why they are always standing in a semicircle
with their arms folded, their bare legs set apart,
their breasts protected by hard metal disks.

DAVID CONSTANTINE

Watching for Dolphins

In the summer months on every crossing to Piraeus
One noticed that certain passengers soon rose
From seats in the packed saloon and with serious
Looks and no acknowledgement of a common purpose
Passed forward through the small door into the bows
To watch for dolphins. One saw them lose

Every other wish. Even the lovers
Turned their desires on the sea, and a fat man
Hung with equipment to photograph the occasion
Stared like a saint, through sad bi-focals; others,
Hopeless themselves, looked to the children for they
Would see dolphins if anyone would. Day after day

Or on their last opportunity all gazed
Undecided whether a flat calm were favourable
Or a sea the sun and the wind between them raised
To a likeness of dolphins. Were gulls a sign, that fell
Screeching from the sky or over an unremarkable place
Sat in a silent school? Every face

After its character implored the sea.
All, unaccustomed, wanted epiphany,
Praying the sky would clang and the abused Aegean
Reverberate with cymbal, gong and drum.
We could not imagine more prayer, and had they then
On the waves, on the climax of our longing come

Smiling, snub-nosed, domed like satyrs, oh
We should have laughed and lifted the children up
Stranger to stranger, pointing how with a leap
They left their element, three or four times, centred
On grace, and heavily and warm re-entered,
Looping the keel. We should have felt them go

Further and further into the deep parts. But soon
We were among the great tankers, under their chains
In black water. We had not seen the dolphins
But woke, blinking. Eyes cast down
With no admission of disappointment the company
Dispersed and prepared to land in the city.

13. AN ASSAY

Our next guest poet is Kate Noakes. Kate is of Welsh blood but her wanderlust has seen her living in Australia, California, South Africa and Paris as well as the UK. Her poetry, as you might expect, is lively, lyrical and global. Kate writes:

Take a look at the following poem from Jane Hirshfield. *Assay* here means to measure the weight, quality, characteristics and so on of a word, rather as one might assay precious metal. You can see this is what Hirshfield is exploring in this poem. Assays have become popular over the last ten years, especially in American poetry. The idea is to do a kind of brainstorming or brain dump – think of all the features, meanings of a thing – a word – and then select and explore these in a poem. Jane Hirshfield is a master of this.

      To have a go yourself, pick one of these words. Simple ones work best for this, and don't spend too long thinking about which one to choose.

RIVER	WATER	STONE	STEEL
GLASS	TREE	FIELD	FISH
FLESH	BREAD	MILK	COFFEE
TEA	TOBACCO	WINE	RAIN
SUN	WIND	SNOW	HAPPINESS
YOUTH	AGE	DEATH	VIOLENCE
HATE	TIME	COTTON	SILK
HAIR	LOVE	SAND	SKY
PALM	POISON	BRIDGE	MOUNTAIN

Then spend ten or fifteen minutes writing down all the things you associate with the word and what it means, what it means to you, when you encountered it, what is conjures up, who it reminds you of and so on. I find a large piece of paper like A3 helps for this mind-mapping (or stick two pieces of A4 together).

Next, start forming the material you have generated into a poem. Something will emerge from even the most unlikely word if you spend long enough considering it.

Enjoy and Good Luck!

JANE HIRSHFIELD

To Judgment: An Assay

You change a life
as eating an artichoke changes the taste
of whatever is eaten after.
Yet you are not an artichoke, not a piano or cat—
not objectively present at all—
and what of you a cat possesses is essential but narrow:
to know if the distance between two things can be leapt.
The piano, that good servant,
has none of you in her at all, she lends herself
to what asks; this has been my ambition as well.
Yet a person who has you is like an iron spigot
whose water comes from far-off mountain springs.
Inexhaustible, your confident pronouncements flow,
coldly delicious.
For if judgment hurts the teeth, it doesn't mind,

not judgment. Teeth pass. Pain passes.
Judgment decrees what remains—
the serene judgments of evolution or the judgment
of a boy-king entering Persia: "Burn it," he says,
and it burns. And if a small tear swells the corner
of one eye, it is only the smoke, it is no more to him than a beetle
fleeing the flames of the village with her six-legged children.
The biologist Haldane—in one of his tenderer moments—
judged beetles especially loved by God,
"because He had made so many." For judgment can be tender:
I have seen you carry a fate to its end as softly as a retriever
carries the quail. Yet however much
I admire you at such moments, I cannot love you:
you are too much in me, weighing without pity your own worth.
When I have erased you from me entirely,
disrobed of your measuring adjectives,
stripped from my shoulders and hips each of your nouns,
when the world is horsefly, coal barge, and dawn the color of
        winter butter—
not *beautiful*, not *cold*, only the color of butter—
then perhaps I will love you. Helpless to not.
As a newborn wolf is helpless: no choice but hunt the wolf milk,
find it sweet.

14. LOST

What have you *lost* lately? Your appetite? Did you lose your faith, your sex drive, your hard drive, the cat, your husband, twenty quid on the horses, twenty pounds on the 5:2 diet? Have you lost interest in the poetry of Elizabeth Bishop – except for her terribly famous poem *One Art*, which is all about loss?

Well, that's all rather depressing.

Loss can, after all, be a joyful thing. Be grateful that you lost that teenage acne or stammer; your crippling shyness, your smoking habit, your virginity – or, like me, a disabling phobia (dogs, since you ask). You may have lost a fear of flying, an appetite for adultery, a beard, a sense of all decorum. Your loss may be a cause for bragging as it was for Jacobean playboy Robert Herrick, overleaf.

No need to tell it in your own voice – you could speak of The Girl Who Lost Her Way Home or The Man Who Lost The Winning Lottery Ticket. For the sake of all our hearts, please steer clear of the lost teddy bear at the supermarket.

Loss often means bereavement. If so, be a little clear-eyed in your grief – this is a big subject and comes with a big pitfall. Resist (always, at all times, in all poems) being merely sentimental or maudlin. Don't focus entirely on your own experience at the expense of the reader's patience. Instead think about the real, complex relationship you had with that person. Remember what irritated you about them. Focus on one or two particular moments, to show us their larger character.

This week's tip – whatever occurs to you immediately is the wrong subject. Too easy, too clichéd. Think for a moment. Avoid the obvious; take a different path. Whatever is on your mind, it will show up in the poem. Trust me on that.

Now go on. Get lost.

ROBERT HERRICK

Upon the Loss of his Mistresses

I have lost, and lately, these
Many dainty mistresses:
Stately Julia, prime of all;
Sappho next, a principal;
Smooth Anthea, for a skin
White, and heaven-like crystalline;
Sweet Electra, and the choice
Myrrha, for the lute, and voice;
Next, Corinna, for her wit,
And the graceful use of it;
With Perilla; all are gone;
Only Herrick's left alone
For to number sorrow by
Their departures hence, and die.

15. BELL, BOOK AND CANDLE

....or kettle, keys and wristwatch. *The unnoticed object* is your subject. Take a close look at the things around you that never normally get a second glance. Read Charles Tomlinson's poem overleaf, looking at a door, or at any of Pablo Neruda's odes to everyday objects like his socks.

Don't choose a souvenir of a special holiday, nor an object already loaded with meaning. Your object should have no immediate significance or memory associated with it. Examine instead the private life of your teapot. Find the hidden stories of a screwdriver. Look at something you never pay attention to. The art of close looking, the trick of paying attention, is half of a poet's job.

The other half, unfortunately, is to express what you've noticed. And there's the rub – how to write about an ordinary and uninteresting thing, without producing an ordinary and uninteresting poem. Go lateral, go whimsical, go deep. Thomas Lux's poem which follows, after all, is about much more than a fridge.

Think sideways about the properties of this ordinary object. What does it DO – tell time, announce guests, offer comfort? How would it speak? Does your mirror know what's behind it, or can it only see forwards?

Tip: Let go. Be led by the object and see where it takes you, rather than deciding what to write about and casting around for an object to fit it. Keep writing. Surprise yourself.

When you're done, read it as if it were someone else's poem. Where does it *really* get going – is the first stanza just telling us what your object is and how you noticed it? Is your first line, perchance, as boring as hell? Bin those lines. Check the last stanza. Is it just saying 'and the moral of the story, children, is...'? Bin those lines.

In fact... why not write about the bin?

CHARLES TOMLINSON

The Door

Too little
has been said
of the door, its one
face turned to the night's
downpour and its other
to the shift and glisten of firelight.

Air, clasped
by this cover
into the room's book,
is filled by the turning
pages of dark and fire
as the wind shoulders the panels, or unsteadies that burning

Not only
the storm's
breakwater, but the sudden
frontier to our concurrences, appearances,
and as the full of the offer of space
as the view through a cromlech is.

For doors
are both frame and monument
to our spent time,
and too little
has been said
of our coming through and leaving by them.

THOMAS LUX

Refrigerator, 1957

More like a vault – you pull the handle out
and on the shelves: not a lot,
and what there is (a boiled potato
in a bag, a chicken carcass
under foil) looking dispirited,
drained, mugged. This is not
a place to go in hope or hunger.
But, just to the right of the middle
of the middle door shelf, on fire, a lit-from-within red,
heart red, sexual red, wet neon red,
shining red in their liquid, exotic,
aloof, slumming
in such company: a jar
of maraschino cherries. Three-quarters
full, fiery globes, like strippers
at a church social. Maraschino cherries, maraschino,
the only foreign word I knew. Not once
did I see these cherries employed: not
in a drink, nor on top
of a glob of ice cream,

or just pop one in your mouth. Not once.
The same jar there through an entire
childhood of dull dinners – bald meat,
pocked peas and, see above,
boiled potatoes. Maybe
they came over from the old country,
family heirlooms, or were status symbols
bought with a piece of the first paycheck
from a sweatshop,
which beat the pig farm in Bohemia,
handed down from my grandparents
to my parents
to be someday mine,
then my child's?
They were beautiful
and, if I never ate one,
it was because I knew it might be missed
or because I knew it would not be replaced
and because you do not eat
that which rips your heart with joy.

16. POETING BY NUMBERS

'Statement: A girl and a boy jump into a river. The boy
swims over to the girl and says, "God, it's cold."
Question: What's the probability they will kiss?'
– Jenny Downham, *You Against Me.*

Probability was never so much fun at my school.
Nonetheless, our theme this week is *numbers*. Note, I
did not say maths; don't panic. Our lives are shaped by
numbers. One in three of us will get cancer. We should eat
five portions of fruit and veg a day, drink two litres of water
a day; hope to live to a hundred.

Pick a number, any number. Like U.A. Fanthorpe
here, you could count the days you have spent with a
partner, or the days since they left. Count the miles between
yourself and your child now living elsewhere, or assess
an impossible number – the stars, the leaves on a tree.
You could consider the numbers you are *not* part of: the
six million Jews who died in the Holocaust; the 3.5 billion
women in the world if you are a man or vice versa; the four
people called Nigel in your night school class.

Count the reasons to be grateful for an April day, or
celebrate every one of the 26 miles in the London Marathon.
Contemplate the fact that you outlived your father at 58,
or passed your driving test on attempt number 3. A phone
number gave you access to Women's Aid or a confused
stranger. Was your life shaped by the fact that you are
Child Number 2 – or were you born as one of three, and
now find yourself one of only two?

How do I love thee? Let me count the ways... oh, there are
at least 52.

U.A. FANTHORPE

7301

Learning to read you, twenty years ago,
Over the pub lunch cheese-and-onion rolls.

Learning how you eat raw onions; learning your taste
For obscurity, how you encode teachers and classrooms

As *the hands, the shop-floor*; learning to hide
The sudden shining naked looks of love. And thinking

The rest of our lives, the rest of our lives
Doing perfectly ordinary things together – riding

In buses, walking in Sainsbury's, sitting
In pubs eating cheese-and-onion rolls.

All those tomorrows. Now twenty years after,
We've had seventy-three hundred of them, and

(If your arithmetic's right, and our luck) we may
Fairly reckon on seventy-three hundred more.

I hold them crammed in my arms, colossal crops
Of shining tomorrows that may never happen,

But may they! Still learning to read you,
To hear what it is you're saying, to master the code.

17. GOING FOR A SONG

Our next guest is one of British poetry's best voices, Matt Merritt. As well as poetry, Matt has written *A Sky Full of Birds*, a guide to great bird gatherings during a year's travels around the British Isles. His prompt, on a natural subject for the editor of a birdwatching magazine, is very different to the one set by our first guest David Morley. Start by reading his own poem, 'Birdsong', overleaf. Matt writes:

Join the dawn chorus. Whether you're waking to the excited chatter of house sparrows in city streets, the rhapsodic improvisations of blackbirds suburban gardens, or the wild, ecstatic trill of curlews on the hills, you can't fail to notice early morning ***birdsong*** at this time of year. Poets have been taking it as their inspiration for centuries.

First, consider why they're singing. To proclaim their territory. To attract a mate. And including both of these, but greater still, to tell the world that they've survived another hard winter, another cold spring night. They sing because they can. Why might *you* be singing?

Next, think about what they're singing. We can't resist the urge to turn birdsong into words – the yellowhammer's 'a little bit of bread and no cheese', or the 'chiff-chaff' that gives one of our commonest warblers its name. Both reproduce the rhythm, but there's still plenty of room for personal interpretations of the actual sounds. Feel free to rewrite even the most widely known of songs, the way that you hear it.

Look at how Alfred, Lord Tennyson's 'The Throstle,' overleaf, imitates the song thrush's habit of repeating phrases two or three times each. Pick a bird, any bird, and let it help you find the rhythm and form of your poem.

Finally, birds have accents and dialects, just like us, and are not above borrowing a choice phrase or two from elsewhere. Starlings are the best everyday example, but you could go the whole hog and emulate the marsh warbler, whose song makes up a map of everywhere they've ever been, and every song they ever heard. Spread your wings a little, and sing.

MATT MERRITT

Birdsong

This evening, a call I don't know,
and will never know, perhaps, drowning
the lisp and whisper of goldcrests
at the edge of the new plantation.

Something hard, metallic, insistent,
but quite distinct from the blackbird,
hammering chinks of light from the dusk
to ward off darkness at this time each night.

Across the street, somebody is yelling
you don't listen. You never listen,
a door's half-heartedly slammed,
and a car radio plays to no one,

but still the unseen bird sings on,
that urgency pitched above
and beyond the background clutter.
Its only sense is now. Is this. Is gone.

The Throstle

'Summer is coming, summer is coming.
   I know it, I know it, I know it.
Light again, leaf again, life again, love again,'
   Yes, my wild little Poet.

Sing the new year in under the blue.
   Last year you sang it as gladly.
'New, new, new, new'! Is it then *so* new
   That you should carol so madly?

'Love again, song again, nest again, young again,'
   Never a prophet so crazy!
And hardly a daisy as yet, little friend,
   See, there is hardly a daisy.

'Here again, here, here, here, happy year'!
   O warble unchidden, unbidden!
Summer is coming, is coming, my dear,
   And all the winters are hidden.

18. NAMING NAMES

'What's in a name? that which we call a rose
By any other name would smell as sweet;
So Romeo would, were he not Romeo call'd,
Retain that dear perfection which he owes
Without that title.' – Shakespeare, *Romeo and Juliet*

Think about *names*. Names are bound up with identity, race and gender, place and power. These are the very words by which we know each other. The names of people, things and places are frames through which we see them.

Start with your own name. What does it give away, or conceal – your ethnicity or class? You may have gained or lost a name through marriage, divorce, adoption or deed poll. If you're a Cohen, you're probably Jewish. If you're a Bell, your ancestors were possibly cattle thieves. Think of a nickname or a pen name, a pet name that only one person ever called you. Sometimes we shake off a loathed name, or chose a new one to fit a self transformed by surgery or faith.

Then again, your choice may not be a personal name at all. It could be a street like Whip-Ma-Whop-Ma-Gate in York or a bird (birds again?) like the Patagonian Tyrant. Your children, your parents, your imaginary friends as a child or those you knew for real – all have resonant names. Revisit an unusual place name, the unwanted ones given to unpopular colleagues or bullied children, the secret ones for fairies which, if divulged, give you power over them. See what stories you end up telling. After all, look where a place name took Edward Thomas.

Tell all. Spill your secrets. Name names.

EDWARD THOMAS

Adlestrop

Yes. I remember Adlestrop—
The name, because one afternoon
Of heat the express-train drew up there
Unwontedly. It was late June.

The steam hissed. Someone cleared his throat.
No one left and no one came
On the bare platform. What I saw
Was Adlestrop—only the name

And willows, willow-herb, and grass,
And meadowsweet, and haycocks dry,
No whit less still and lonely fair
Than the high cloudlets in the sky.

And for that minute a blackbird sang
Close by, and round him, mistier,
Farther and farther, all the birds
Of Oxfordshire and Gloucestershire.

19. FIRSTLY

Start with Sharon Olds' poem, opposite.

Now, don't panic. I am not asking you to write about sex; not this week, anyway. Our nineteenth prompt is *the first time.*

Write about the first time you did something. It should be something which you have done many times since – something which subsequently became very familiar, so that the first time will cast its light forward onto every later occasion. The first time you ate an olive or smoked a cigarette; wrote your name, rode a motorbike, painted your nails, fixed a car, broke a heart.

Get right back into that moment and remember how it felt. Be as you were *then,* not as you are now – remember the surprise, what you expected the experience to be like, how it actually was. Were you good at it immediately, or did you have to practice?

You might start from an important activity that defines your experience. Perhaps you have spent years intervening to correct racist statements; perhaps you have spent years ignoring them, and can remember the first time you decided to do that. Perhaps you are an Alcoholics Anonymous member or a Quaker; what was the first meeting like? Humbler moments have significance too. Opening the door to your own flat for the first time or boiling the perfect three-minute egg are both memorable firsts.

As always, occupying another voice can be a useful way in. Roger Bannister's four-minute mile, a duckling taking to water for the first time, a gangster's first killing... these will all give you (and your reader) pause for thought.

Don't end with 'and that was just the first of many...' We get that. You wouldn't be telling unless it meant something.

You're a poet, after all.

SHARON OLDS

First Sex

I knew little, and what I knew
I did not believe – they had lied to me
so many times, so I just took it as it
came, his naked body on the sheet,
the tiny hairs curling on his legs like
fine, gold shells, his sex
harder and harder under my palm
and yet not hard as a rock his face cocked
back as if in terror, the sweat
jumping out of his pores like sudden
trails from the tiny snails when his knees
locked with little clicks and under my
hand he gathered and shook and the actual
flood like milk came out of his body, I
saw it glow on his belly, all they had
said and more, I rubbed it into my hands
like lotion, I signed on for the duration.

20. IS THAT AN EPISTLE IN YOUR POCKET, OR....?

Dear poet:

We used to write letters. We wrote to lovers, to friends, to prospective employers. We wrote to children at boarding school and soldiers on service, to elderly relatives who sent us Christmas gifts we didn't want. We sent letters of advice. Doing research once, I found a letter from Isambard Kingdom Brunel to a stroppy customer who had dared to complain that his order (a boat of Brunel's design) was late. The great engineer signed off with this magnificent flourish of temper –

'I am, sir, your obedient servant. And if you were mine, I should give you a damn good flogging'.

Nowadays the scarcity of physical letters lends them a sense of occasion. Join the tradition of epistolary poets – writing *a poem in the form of a letter.* Letters are vivid, personal, revealing.

Don't write a poem *about* a letter. This poem should *be* a letter, because that gives you instant access to its immediacy and a more intimate register of language. Write to a particular addressee – for moral instruction, for amusement, for catharsis, for the hell of it. Make it angry and accusatory, in a letter to a politician or a burglar (they're different, honestly). Make it sexy and serious, in a letter to your lover coming home after a month away. Make it whimsical and mindful, or deep and instructive. Write to Martin Luther King, the Buddha or your sixteen-year old self.

Whoever your addressee is, let us know – but

remember that in a letter to your closest childhood friend Tibby, you would never say 'Dear Tibby, you were my closest childhood friend'. Resist exposition. Make it clear in some other way, perhaps in the title. Write with your own rhythms, your own tics and phrases (or, if you write in another voice, invent convincing tics).

Oh, and one other thing.

Mean it.

Kind Regards,
    Jo Bell.

HAYDEN CARRUTH

The Afterlife: Letter to Sam Hamill

You may think it strange, Sam, that I'm writing
a letter in these circumstances. I thought
it strange too—the first time. But there's
a misconception I was laboring under, and you
are too, viz. that the imagination in your
vicinity is free and powerful. After all,
you say, you've been creating yourself all
along imaginatively. You imagine yourself
playing golf or hiking in the Olympics or
writing a poem and then it becomes true.
But you still have to do it, you have to exert
yourself, will, courage, whatever you've got, you're
mired in the unimaginative. Here I imagine a letter
and it's written. Takes about two-fifths of a
second, your time. Hell, this is heaven, man.

I can deluge Congress with letters telling
every one of those mendacious sons of bitches
exactly what he or she is, in maybe about
half an hour. In spite of your Buddhist
proclivities, when you imagine bliss
you still must struggle to get there. By the way
the Buddha has his place across town on
Elysian Drive. We call him Bud. He's lost weight
and got new dentures, and he looks a hell of a
lot better than he used to. He always carries
a jumping jack with him everywhere just
for contemplation, but he doesn't make it
jump. He only looks at it. Meanwhile Sidney
and Dizzy, Uncle Ben and Papa Yancey, are
over by Sylvester's Grot making the sweetest,
cheerfulest blues you ever heard. The air,
so called, is full of it. Poems are fluttering
everywhere like seed from a cottonwood tree.
Sam, the remarkable truth is I can do any
fucking thing I want. Speaking of which
there's this dazzling young Naomi who
wiped out on I-80 just west of Truckee
last winter, and I think this is the moment
for me to go and pay her my respects.
Don't go way. I'll be right back.

21. ANT MUSIC

'If we were to wipe out insects alone on this planet, the rest of life and humanity with it would mostly disappear from the land. Within a few months.'
– E.O. Wilson

'I don't care how small or big they are, insects freak me out.' – Alexander Wang

There is poetry everywhere, even in the dung heap. *Insects* buzz and flutter and sting the air around us. They have us outnumbered us and will outlast us. They thrive in every evolutionary niche – from the bluebottle, living on excrement and unpopular in the kitchen, to the Wandering Violin Mantis (yes, really). If it has six legs or eight, it's fair game for us this week. Consider the astonishing life cycle of the caddis fly, or the philosophy of the wasp. Explore what it's like to grow up in a chrysalis.

You may want to do some research. Is it true that ants make up two-thirds of the biomass of insects in the world or that anatomically, the bumblebee shouldn't be able to fly? Why was the scarab beetle held sacred in ancient Egypt? Mine the rich language of a field guide for facts and proper names. Look at folklore about insects (but go steady on those Telling the Bees poems, they are common as flies).

Above all, pay attention. All good poems begin with close observation – but to be interesting for a reader, it needs to be more than that. As Thoreau said, 'the question is not what you look at but what you see'. So Tony Hoagland, overleaf, renders a moment with an insect as both meaningful and innocent without sounding trite. Use your insect as a metaphor, as an incidental character in a bigger story, or as the centre of the universe.

After all, Kafka did alright out of it.

TONY HOAGLAND

Field Guide

Once, in the cool blue middle of a lake,
up to my neck in that most precious element of all,

I found a pale-gray, curled-upwards pigeon feather
floating on the tension of the water

at the very instant when a dragonfly,
like a blue-green iridescent bobby pin,

hovered over it, then lit, and rested.
That's all.

I mention this in the same way
that I fold the corner of a page

in certain library books,
so that the next reader will know

where to look for the good parts.

22. PURPLE PROSE

Our guest poet here is Luke Kennard. Prolific, funny, fiercely intelligent and charming, his work is fresh and inventive; sometimes unsettling, always a stimulant to the poetry palate. He is particularly known for his prose poetry. If this prompt makes you uncomfortable – *good*. Stick with it; it's good to get out of your comfort zone whenever you can. Luke writes:

Put simply, if a free verse poem does away with strict rhyme and metre, *a prose poem* also does away with line-break. That's a very negative way of looking at it, of course, and it may be more edifying to consider the possibilities the form allows. Shorn of any other outward manifestation of the poetic, we're left with imagery alone.

Most prose poems look like little paragraphs of prose (see my own piece, which follows). Charles Baudelaire was arguably the first poet to use (and name) the form in the 1860s, in a collection called *Paris Spleen*. No, I have no idea why he thought they were poems either, even after writing a thesis on the subject. The form became popular on the Continent and in the US, but didn't take off in the UK because T.S. Eliot (after writing one vaguely misogynistic prose poem called 'Hysteria') declared that he despised it. Up-and-coming writers tended to want to stay on his good side.

One way of introducing extra form to the proceedings is to impose a template on the prose: complete the sentences and repeat the pattern to create a sequence of variations. This is an exercise I often use when I'm introducing the idea of form and pattern to a new class. I also use it myself when I'm feeling low in confidence, which is most of the time. Like any form, it has the advantage of forcing your hand, unearthing thoughts and ideas you didn't know you had. Here's my starter template:

> When I reached the edge of the desert I saw…
> You told me…
> I couldn't…
> It was as if…

The first sentence asks for some physical description, the second and third introduce a companion and possible conflict, the fourth asks for some kind of analogy to sum up. I set a minute or two to complete each sentence, then a further 5-10 minutes to write out two variations using the same template. Some of the best results come from the writer trying to link together a kind of narrative between the three variations. As I said, this is a starter-template, so the real challenge is to come up with your own sentence/ word pattern to repeat and work with.

LUKE KENNARD

GERALD VARIATIONS

Maybe you have an empty room to charter to his likeness; but you do not know this Gerald by whom I am enthralled – because he renovates my mind with his very presence like a hardback anthology of insights I dip into whenever I am bedridden by a head-cold. And unfortunately asking him about it is out of the question.

Maybe you have a missing button that fell into the bouillabaisse; but you do not know this Gerald whom I cannot stand – for the esoteric arrogance of his every utterance is like a vital ritual in an obscure and terrifying religion. And unfortunately he is not here to defend himself.

Maybe you have exaggerated the dubious moral relativism of your township's museum; but you do not know this Gerald to whom I am indifferent – for his trespasses have come to disappoint me, like the overstated hallucinogenic properties of a harmless dried root. And unfortunately I have spent all the money intended for utility bills.

Maybe you have recorded an album with a caged seagull and two agnostic percussionists; but you do not know this Gerald whom I love – for I have known the fiscal security of his patronage like a doctor's hand against my heart. And unfortunately he will not extend the same courtesy to you.

Maybe you have manufactured and sold a range of oblivion-flavoured sweets; but you do not know this Gerald whom I loathe – for I have felt the humiliation of his scorn like fat spitting from a frying pan or fireworks in a celebration against me. And unfortunately I was too taken aback to retaliate.

Maybe you have had sex on a bicycle without sustaining or bestowing a single injury; but you do not know this Gerald with whom I am currently eating a hot dog – because we are both hungry. And unfortunately I have dripped mustard onto his copy of *The Cloud of Unknowing*.

Maybe you have sought his face in cross-sections of courgette; but you do not know this Gerald to whom I am currently dealing little deaths – because I trod in dog excrement on my way back from the post office. And unfortunately I am wearing shoes with an especially deep tread.

Maybe you have skipped across the rocks and broken your leg on an abandoned rowing boat; but you do not know this Gerald to whom I feel superior – as for all his intelligence, he has forsaken his humility and humours my ideas like a cat toying with a shrew. And unfortunately the irony of the situation is lost on me.

23. GREAT LIVES

Of all the prompts I used in the 52 blog where this book began, it was this innocent little piece that caused most consternation. I still don't understand why. Perhaps people felt that it was a test of their historical knowledge. It isn't, so don't be afraid.

Your 23rd mission is to **write about a historic figure** in whom you have an interest. You don't have to admire them. Choose a person who is:

> a) **real**
> b) **famous**
> c) **dead**

Einstein or Beethoven, Hitler or Gandhi, Maya Angelou or Bobby Moore, Catherine the Great or Haile Selassie – whomever you choose, it does need to be a famous person, not a person in your own life. That person is your subject.

It's hard to write about these figures without overloading them, hanging virtues around their neck like flowery millstones. It's hard to avoid polemic or 'and-so-she-showed-us-that-War-Is-A-Very-Bad-Thing' triteness. You don't want to write a short, worshipful biography, which does nothing more thought-provoking than an entry on Wikipedia. How to avoid all that? I offer you two tips – which you may disregard of course.

First, concentrate on *one* incident. Gandhi weaves the piece of homespun cloth which he sent to Elizabeth II as a wedding present. Neil Armstrong steps onto the Moon; Joan of Arc steps out to the pyre. Remember too that we are after truth, not accuracy. Just because you have discovered a series of fascinating facts about Frida Kahlo, you don't have to cram them *all* in.

Second tip: take a point of view which shows us the person as an ordinary human. Put your subject in a domestic setting, as Kinnell did with Keats back in Week 4. One very good way to make someone less godlike (in poetry, as in life) is to marry them as Carol Ann Duffy does, below. The very best way to make someone human is to *become* them. Be Marie Antoinette at the banquet, Freud buying cigars.

No, forget that last one. It will only lead to trouble.

CAROL ANN DUFFY

Anne Hathaway

'Item I gyve unto my wief my second best bed…'
(from Shakespeare's will)

The bed we loved in was a spinning world
of forests, castles, torchlight, cliff-tops, seas
where he would dive for pearls. My lover's words
were shooting stars which fell to earth as kisses
on these lips; my body now a softer rhyme
to his, now echo, assonance; his touch
a verb dancing in the centre of a noun.
Some nights I dreamed he'd written me, the bed
a page beneath his writer's hands. Romance
and drama played by touch, by scent, by taste.
In the other bed, the best, our guests dozed on,
dribbling their prose. My living laughing love –
I hold him in the casket of my widow's head
as he held me upon that next best bed.

24. I CAN SEE A RAINBOW

'Colour is my day-long obsession, joy and torment'
– Claude Monet

Colour is present everywhere: at the fruit market, in the crazy colour-bombs of Holi and even in illness and death. In Dannie Abse's poem which follows, it is the precisely named colours that do the visual and emotional work. Yet the same kaleidoscope of refracted light gives us yellow sunflowers, red wine and the jewel box majesty of the Sainte Chapelle.

Write about colour (but preferably *not* skin colour, which exercises different poetry muscles and is not for this week). This is a wide-ranging, enough-rope-to-hang-yourself with prompt. There are lots of ways to tackle it.

You might want to pick a single colour and pursue it through all its manifestations. Write a list of the blues you know (your father's eyes, the mould in Stilton, the Adriatic, the Facebook button). Enumerate the shades of green in an English hedgerow; the many kinds of white in an Antarctic landscape or hospital waiting room; the outlandishly named colours on a Farrow & Ball paint chart. Every colour carries a host of meanings – back in prompt 10, Kim Addonizio got full-throated, red-blooded value out of a red dress. Colour is used as metaphor – you're in the pink or seeing red, singing the blues, black-hearted or green-thumbed, troubled by the green-eyed monster.

Your subject, as ever, is not purely the object you're describing but the way we see it, the way it makes us look a little differently at the world. A poem is never about what it's about.

Pitfall alert: those Technicolor words like *vermilion, indigo, burnt umber* are luscious on the tongue but sound far too florid for most poetry. Use them sparingly, to enhance your palette of primary colours. Homer famously spoke of 'the wine-dark sea' to convey its colour. In this and many other subjects, the simple word is often the most effective.

Red. Purple. White.
Paint yourself into a corner.

DANNIE ABSE

Pathology of Colours

I know the colour rose, and it is lovely,
but not when it ripens in a tumour;
and healing greens, leaves and grass, so springlike,
in limbs that fester are not springlike.

I have seen red-blue tinged with hirsute mauve
in the plum-skin face of a suicide.
I have seen white, china white almost, stare
from behind the smashed windscreen of a car.

And the criminal, multi-coloured flash
of an H-bomb is no more beautiful
than an autopsy when the belly's opened –
to show cathedral windows never opened.

So in the simple blessing of a rainbow,
in the bevelled edge of a sunlit mirror,
I have seen, visible, Death's artefact
like a soldier's ribbon on a tunic tacked.

25. NOISES OFF

Listen. *Listen*. What can you hear, right now?

I'm typing this in my narrow boat. As I type I hear my fingers tapping on the keys, and ducks tapping on the hull; the engines of other boats chugging past, the lock gear clattering as they work their way up or down the canal. There is the quiet openness of water and trees, but also the loud rattle and honk of a train at the level crossing, the tick of a steel hull cooling after a hot day.

I *can't* hear a cat, a husband running a bath, a teenager playing with an iPad. I *can't* hear gunfire or Niagara Falls, or anyone snoring, as described here in the following poem by Josh Ekroy. But all these sounds are out there, somewhere. Write, then, about sounds. Church bells or school bells, the beep of the smoke alarm running out of battery, the jingle of your computer as it starts up, the remembered sound of an old car, the roar of a football crowd...

Listen to the world around you. Start now. Seriously. Close your eyes and begin to hear all the things you normally filter out. Even the simplest sound can be a gateway to something extraordinary and wise.

Look again at Edward Thomas's 'Adlestrop' from Week 18. That poem endures partly because of a subtle finish which cocks the reader's ear, leading you out from the platform to listen for yourself.

What can you hear? Listen.

JOSH EKROY

Barracks Snorers

I wake at three a.m., shift my weight
onto my back; did I hear a storm?
I listen, realise how the snared beat
of their engines has hijacked my dreams.
I've travelled to their rhythms, wrestled
with the hooting agents of their junta,
seen their air-grabs and misfired missiles.
I lie there, stilled by their bluster,
– is that Shostakovich giving birth? –
jump at a snort of indignation, give a start
at the rallying whistles of breath,
the after-loss of freighted effort.

These blokes are nothing like this
when awake; they claim life stands
at ease before them, and though their eyes
deny they've anything to defend,
here they attack, pause, struggle.
How deeply they commit to sleep,
how primally they appeal from it, wriggling
their feet, playing cavemen's pipes.
Their pith is dragged from them in fits,
wheezed air bellowsed out in pangs,
teasing and snagging the glottis,
the stored discourse of dry tongues.

26 – WRITTEN ON THE BODY

Our guest poet for this halfway marker point is Neil Rollinson. Wholly engaging, wholeheartedly physical, startlingly honest and deep, Neil's poetry pulls no punches on any subject. He is one of our boldest and best contemporary writers. Neil writes:

I'm writing this at midsummer. We're all hot under the collar. I know what's on your mind! Yes, the birds and the bees, so let's repair to our boudoirs and pen a little *erotica*. Before we begin, let's lie back and consider a few pointers. This is a subject rife with cliché. It is all too easy to get over-excited and before you know it, your poems are more like a Mills & Boon love-in, with all manner of heaving manhood and palpitating hearts. We need to look at this with a fresh eye. So calm down, get a cold shower, put on a clean shirt and let's begin. As Wordsworth said, poetry is emotion recollected in tranquillity; and that's a good start for those of us with an erotic bent. Let's try and come at this from a different angle, a fresh angle.

Let's write an erotic poem that's about other issues: illness, growing old, familial and domestic disappointment perhaps. Does that sound promising? Well, Deborah Harding does exactly this in her marvellous poem 'Baseball in the Living Room', overleaf.

Not only is it fiercely honest in its eroticism, that wonderful lustiness, it is also a heart-breaking poem, about her parents. And funny to boot. A good ruse of course is to let something else carry the focus, or energy, and let the erotic take a back seat. Whatever you're doing though, whatever you're writing about, you must seek to deepen the experience of the poem. Superficial or one-dimensional poems are never successful, but you know that already.

So that's one way of doing it, but we can also write in a more direct way about sex, perhaps from our own perspectives, but this is a much harder ask. We live in prurient times, and you could be asking for trouble, so make it as good as you can, steer clear of any cliché – I can't stress that enough – and make it fresh and original, even funny, if you can. My advice would be this: *be serious*. Flippancy in matters of sex always looks bad. You can be as explicit as you like, so don't worry about that – many of my own poems have been noted for their explicit nature, like the one opposite: but don't be gratuitous. Be honest. All experience comes from the same wellspring. If you are being honest in your telling, then we as readers will recognise that, and empathise. My poems are anecdotal and knowing in their way, which helps to keep a distance between myself and my subject; a similar approach, though much more powerful, is the confessional. For my money, Sharon Olds' 'First Sex' is one of the best. (Look back at Week 19 to see it again.)

It doesn't get much better than that. It is graphic in its way, but also lyrical. You can feel its sincerity. It is both honest and celebratory, both qualities that will help your poem relate and endure, and lyricism of course will always elevate the tone of anything you write about.

Then there's the humorous. For this I'd go in search of Catherine Smith's poem 'Losing it to David Cassidy'; it's seamlessly sexy and funny, it's difficult to write a poem this good.

Right, let's get going. The key here, as always is originality, clarity, focus and precision of imagery. Avoid abstraction, concentrate on concrete nouns, and avoid cliché like the plague, which is itself a whopping great cliché. Good luck.

DEBORAH HARDING ALLBRITAIN

Baseball in the Living Room

Through the yellow roses on the coffee table
I peer at the ball game, tired of Whitman, tired
of wanting to be great.

"Holy cow," roars the announcer,
"walk him walk him," Dad hollers,
my parents planted in their twin recliners, suited up
in silk pajamas – and when it's Miller time Dad
limps to the kitchen with his bad hip, there's the chink
of spoon and glass as he mixes the nightly dose of meta-mucil –
Mom turns to me with that sigh of surrender:
"since the surgery," she says,
"all he wants to do is watch baseball."
Five to three. Top of the eighth.
Leary pitching.
"Who do you think our pin-up boy's gonna be this year?"
jokes one of the guys – and I stare at these beauties,
the hard butts, the kind
you want to sink your nails into.

The first baseman slides one hand
over his hip, wets his bottom lip –
I think he wants me
then the black one leans over the plate
ready to swing – he means business, that look
you want to see when a man's
on top of you – these men in their prime,
I'd take any one of them
right now on this couch – Dad snoring,
I should go to bed, finish The Body Electric, sleep...

Gonzales fouls one,
spits a stream of tobacco, a thick gold chain ribs
his neck like a rein, wild eyes

dark as river stone —
Mom's drifting now, her head makes little bobs
before she catches it
somewhere in a field of consciousness.

Berryhill slams it to third, the crowd
leaps to their feet — everyone's going nuts,
the full moon, my bare legs, the ball low and outside.

NEIL ROLLINSON

Like the Blowing of Birds' Eggs

I crack the shell
on the bedstead and open it
over your stomach. It runs
to your navel and settles there
like the stone of a sharon fruit.

You ask me to gather it up
and pour it over your breast
without breaking the membrane.

It swims in my palm, drools
from the gaps in my fingers, fragrant,
spotted with blood.

It slips down your chest,
moves on your skin like a woman
hurrying in her yellow dress, the long
transparent train dragging behind.

It slides down your belly and into your
pubic hair where you burst
the yolk with a tap of your finger.

It covers your cunt in a shock
of gold. You tell me to eat,
to feel the sticky glair on my tongue.

I lick the folds of your sex, the coarse
damp hairs, the slopes of your arse
until you're clean, and tense as a clock spring.

I touch your spot and something inside you
explodes like the blowing of birds' eggs.

27. SAYING SORRY

What do you say when you tread on someone's toe – or, if you are English, when they tread on your toe? You use the word we use to end a relationship or a world war. Opposite is Glyn Maxwell with an apparently sincere apology, but we often say it insincerely or sarcastically – 'I'm sorry, but I disagree', 'I'm sorry, but you'll just have to park somewhere else'. When spoken from the heart, it can be a large word indeed.

Say sorry to someone. This, incidentally, is about 'sorry' in the sense of a direct apology – not feeling sorry for someone, or being generally sorry about the state of the world.

Make a long-overdue apology for that thing you did. Yes, *that* thing. When you stole little Bobby's tractor at playschool, or slept with Natalya's husband; when you said something wrong, and swiftly glossed over it, but never stopped wishing you had apologised. Apologise for queue-jumping or adultery, for shoplifting those socks from Top Shop in 1982, or for the great historic wrongs you were not actually responsible for. Say sorry to your wife for not bringing her breakfast in bed. As ever, keep it specific rather than general – use a particular incident as a hook to hang the poem on. Being sorry implies shame, and shame is difficult. Let it show.

If you are a saintly type who has never done anything to apologise for, or the sort of git who never apologises, or an Edith Piaf type singing *je ne regrette rien*, then make an angry or insincere apology. If you can't face up to your own mistakes at all, then apologise for someone else. Julius Caesar apologises for conquering Britannia. Pope Joan apologises for fibbing about her gender.

Now... go to your room. And don't come down till you're ready to say sorry.

GLYN MAXWELL

Deep Sorriness Atonement Song

(for missed appointment, BBC North, Manchester)

The man who sold Manhattan for a halfway decent bangle,
He had talks with Adolf Hitler and could see it from his angle,
And he could have signed the Quarrymen but didn't think
    they'd make it
So he bought a cake on Pudding Lane and thought "Oh well
    I'll bake it"

But his chances they were slim
And his brothers they were Grimm,
And he's sorry, very sorry,
But I'm sorrier than him.

And the drunken plastic surgeon who said "I know, let's
    enlarge 'em!"
And the bloke who told the Light Brigade "Oh what the hell,
    let's charge 'em",
The magician with an early evening gig on the Titanic
And the Mayor who told the people of Atlantis not to panic,

And the Dong about his nose
And the Pobble re his toes,
They're all sorry, very sorry
But I'm sorrier than those.

And don't forget the Bible, with the Sodomites and Judas,
And Onan who discovered something nothing was as rude as,
And anyone who reckoned it was City's year for Wembley.
And the kid who called Napoleon a shortarse in assembly,

And the man who always smiles
Cause he knows I have his files,
They're all sorry, really sorry,
But I'm sorrier by miles.

And Robert Falcon Scott who lost the race to the Norwegian,
And anyone who's ever split a pint with a Glaswegian,
Or told a Finn a joke or spent an hour with a Swiss-German,
Or got a mermaid in the sack and found it was a merman,

Or him who smelt a rat,
And got curious as a cat,
They're all sorry, deeply sorry,
But I'm sorrier than that.

All the people who were rubbish when we needed them to do it,
Whose wires crossed, whose spirit failed, who ballsed it up or
    blew it,
All notches of nul points and all who have a problem Houston,
At least they weren't in Kensington when they should have been
    at Euston.

For I didn't build the Wall
And I didn't cause the Fall
But I'm sorry, Lord, I'm sorry,
I'm the sorriest of all.

28. STOP ALL THE CLOCKS

Time flies, whether you're having fun or not. And *time* is a hard subject to tackle; one of those Grand Themes which can go wrong in grand style. It is, after all, infinite. There are so many ways to approach it that you can end up with a grandiose failure.

The key to avoiding that booby trap, as we've seen so many times in these prompts, is to balance specificity and generality. In the immortal words of friend Norman Hadley, 'your poem must be about left handed widgets but also about Everything.' A poem has to be specific enough for us to believe in the writer's experience – but general enough for the reader to find it relevant, interesting, useful in negotiating a path through the world.

This prompt, then, is *not* about time in general – but about *a particular time of day,* a specific time on the clock. Think first about your own routines. Do you do the same thing at eight o'clock every day – make the coffee, put the radio on, pray? Or does the time stick in your mind because something terribly significant happened one day at that hour? The time may might be central to the telling, or it might be mentioned only as a detail in the larger picture, as Fleur Adcock does overleaf.

Make an appointment to meet your lover, your optician, your cancer specialist. Notice that the clock stopped at ten to three, and ask yourself why. Remember the silence at 11.00 a.m. on Armistice Day, or consider the small horrors of the 3.00 p.m. school run.

Get writing. The clock is ticking...

FLEUR ADCOCK

Counting

You count the fingers first: it's traditional.
(You assume the doctor counted them too,
when he lifted up the slimy surprise
with its long dark pointed head and its father's nose
at 2.13 a.m. – 'Look at the clock!'
said Sister: 'Remember the time: 2.13.')

Next day the head's turned pink and round;
the nose is a blob. You fumble under the gown
your mother embroidered with a sprig of daisies,
as she embroidered your own Viyella gowns
when you were a baby. You fish out
curly triangular feet. You count the toes.

'There's just one little thing' says Sister:
'His ears – they don't quite match. One
has an extra whorl in it. No one will notice.'
You notice like mad. You keep on noticing.
Then you hear a rumour: a woman in the next ward
has had a stillbirth. Or was it something worse?

You lie there, bleeding gratefully.
You've won the Nobel Prize, and the VC,
and the State Lottery, and gone to heaven.
Feed-time comes. They bring your bundle –
the right one: it's him all right.
You count his eyelashes: the ideal number.

You take him home. He learns to walk.
From time to time you eye him,
nonchalantly, from each side.
He has an admirable nose.
No one ever notices his ears. No one
ever stands on both sides of him at once.

He grows up. He has beautiful children.

29. THE PROVERBIAL

In these islands, our daily speech groans under the weight of *proverbs and quotations*. We're laden with idioms, sayings and epigrams so well-worn as to be part of our daily language – ancient proverbs from the Bible, lines from Shakespeare, memes from Facebook. The best ones chew over the wisdom of the ages and spit it out as a memorable nugget of useful advice.

Pick one and run with it. If you can't think of any right now, start listening out for them – they bubble up everywhere. *Once bitten, twice shy. Be careful what you wish for. A fool and his money are soon parted. Many hands make light work. Don't look a gift horse in the mouth.* If you get stuck, look online for a list of proverbs – perhaps from another culture. Even if we don't know the proverb, we might be able to deduce it from the poem, as with A.E. Stallings' poem opposite.

If you don't fancy the proverbial, then start from a famous quotation: Burke's 'The only thing necessary for the triumph of evil is for good men to do nothing,' or the Dalai Lama's 'Be kind whenever possible. It is always possible.' Remember or invent a moment that illustrates it.

Pitfall alert: if you rely too heavily on the phrase itself, your poem is likely to become vague and pompous. The proverb is the spark for your piece, not the punchline. In fact, you needn't include the saying in the poem at all. It could be the title, or an epigraph. Take liberties – this is a great exercise in trusting your reader, who knows the language just as well as you do.

A.E. STALLINGS

After a Greek Proverb

Ουδέν μονιμότερον του προσωρινού

We're here for the time being, I answer to the query—
Just for a couple of years, we said, a dozen years back.
Nothing is more permanent than the temporary.

We dine sitting on folding chairs—they were cheap but cheery.
We've taped the broken window pane. TV's still out of whack.
We're here for the time being, I answer to the query.

When we crossed the water, we only brought what we could carry,
But there are always boxes that you never do unpack.
Nothing is more permanent than the temporary.

Sometimes when I'm feeling weepy, you propose a theory:
Nostalgia and tear gas have the same acrid smack.
We're here for the time being, I answer to the query—

We stash bones in the closet when we don't have time to bury,
Stuff receipts in envelopes, file papers in a stack.
Nothing is more permanent than the temporary.

Twelve years now and we're still eating off the ordinary:
We left our wedding china behind, afraid that it might crack.
We're here for the time being, we answer to the query,
But nothing is more permanent than the temporary.

30. WITH FRIENDS LIKE THESE

Your theme this time around is a pleasant one: *time with friends*. A friend you see often, or one you haven't seen for years (like Chris Beckett, writing in the Ethiopian tradition of praise poems, opposite). One who is lost to you through death or distance; one who lives next door. *Not*, please, one who happens also to be your mother or your husband. Keep it platonic, eh?

Remember an extraordinary or ordinary moment with them. Don't try to make it Mean Something. It already means something. Get right inside it. Remember what was on the stereo, how bad the restaurant was, how a friend helped you through chemo or tap dancing classes. Try addressing it to the friend directly, for the same immediacy as our epistolary poems in Week 20.

Fill it with love and keep it concrete, physical. If your particular memory is mournful, then slow it down with vowel sounds like *oh* and *ah* – if a motorbike ride, keep it fast with consonants and short vowels.

Then phone a friend. Poems, even the best of them, are only representations of the important stuff.

CHRIS BECKETT

Abebe, the cook's son!

Abebe, from a distant afternoon
Abebe, from an afternoon where everybody naps
even the donkeys propped against trees
    on their little hoofs
Abebe, tall as a eucalyptus tree
Abebe, black all over when he pisses on a eucalyptus tree
who jaunties me down dirt tracks to the honey shop
    buys two drippy honeycombs in a box
Abebe, the cool one in drain-pipe jeans and sky-blue sneakers
Abebe, the busy crossing where girls stop to chat
who clicks his fingers to the funky Ibex Band
    as we slow-boy back up track
Abebe, calling *come here!* to the dog called Come Here
Abebe, trotting round the dogyard like a horse
who saddles up the smokey horses and takes me galloping
who shouts at mud-caves where hyenas sleep
who shows me how to make *kwalima* beef and ginger sausages
    and a happy chick-pea fish for Lent
Abebe, gobbling up the afternoon like a *kwalima*
Abebe, grinning like a chick-pea fish
    while everybody naps

31. HOME SWEET HOME?

Our seventh guest poet is Angela France. Her own work is full of meditations on womanhood, nature and change. She also serves the poetry community as part of the editorial team at respected journal *Iota* and founder of the long-running poetry reading night *Buzzwords*. Angela writes:

Think of the place you think of as *home*, whether actual or spiritual. Is there a single quality you associate with it? A word that captures its essence?

We are always told, in poetry, to avoid the abstract and use concrete detail but for this part of the prompt, abstract qualities may be what comes to mind. You may think of a mood, a quality of light, a temperature, a type of weather; or, as in the case of Sheryl St. Germain's poem opposite, a pace.

See how she turns the whole poem into a meditation on *'slow'*. She uses the long, languorous lines to reinforce the slowness, how her word choices and vowel sounds are slow and rich. The poem reads as a celebration of New Orleans's slowness – or does it? One reader in a workshop thought it reads as a complaint about the frustration and claustrophobia of the slowness; the quality you associate with home may not be a positive one.

Martin Figura's poem 'Piggotts', also following, uses lists and long lines but to entirely different effect. The Piggotts were the large, rowdy, chaotic family who rescued Martin from a children's home. The words breathlessly tumble over each other, not only evoking but invoking an overwhelming atmosphere of chaos and warmth. The verbs, often beginning a sentence, drive this poem with unstoppable energy; from just the first few lines – *bashing clouting jammed flying dragged thrown*. Phew!

In both poems, the details are specific and concrete so that the reader can fully enter into the world evoked.

So, off you go. Have fun!

SHERYL ST. GERMAIN

Going Home: New Orleans
for my grandmother, Theresa Frank

Some slow evenings when the light hangs late and
    stubborn in the sky,
gives itself up to darkness slowly and deliberately, slow
    cloud after slow cloud,
slowness enters me like something familiar,
and it feels like going home.

It's all there in the disappearing light:
all the evenings of slow sky and slow loving, slow boats on
    sluggish bayous;
the thick-middled trees with the slow-sounding names—
    oak, mimosa, pecan, magnolia;
the slow tree sap that sticks in your hair when you lie with
    the trees;
and the maple syrup and pancakes and grits, the butter
    melting

slowly into and down the sides like sweat between breasts
    of sloe-eyed strippers;
and the slow-throated blues that floats over the city like fog;
and the weeping, the willows, the cut onions, the cayenne,
the slow-cooking beans with marrow-thick gravy;
and all the mint juleps drunk so slowly on all the slow
    southern porches,
the bourbon and sugar and mint going down warm and
    brown, syrup and slow;
and all the ice cubes melting in all the iced teas,
all the slow-faced people sitting in all the slowly rocking
    rockers;
and the crabs and the shrimp and crawfish, the hard shells
slowly and deliberately and lovingly removed, the delicate
    flesh
slowly sucked out of heads and legs and tails;
and the slow lips that eat and drink and love and speak
that slow luxurious language, savoring each word like a
    long-missed lover;
and the slow-moving nuns, the black habits dragging the
    swollen ground;
and the slow river that cradles it all, and the chicory coffee
that cuts through it all, slow-boiled and black as dirt;
and the slow dreams and the slow-healing wounds and the
    slow smoke of it all
slipping out, ballooning into the sky—slow, deliberate, and
    magnificent.

Piggotts

Taken prisoner by this bashing clouting clan. Jammed between
Danny and John, the second and third boys with their shock
white hair and flying fists. Dragged through lanes and hedges
into ponds and up trees for birds' eggs. Thrown into the gritty-
eyed dawn for mushrooms as big as dinner plates and damsons
for damson jam. Put to work with sandpaper on rusting scrap-
heap cars. Flying over fields on the Honda Fifty, being chased
by the mad dog. The mad dog burying bones in your bed;
hurling itself downstairs, sticking its head up women's skirts.
Dianne as look-out while we skinny dip in the River Weaver
and once a water-rat swam between us. Dianne goes to
the Grammar; Billy crashed his Lambretta and then his Capri,
went to Spain with his mates.

Holidays on Shell Island – *famous for its shells* – :
pitching into the air off dunes, racing the tide, screaming from
cliff tops, hauling crabs from the sea on twine on pop bottles,
diving into waves, digging a tunnel in the sand, me buried
alive, recovering in the tent's strange orange light listening to
Day of The Triffids on the radio.

Friday night with Woodpecker Cider watching the
Hammer Horror film, falling asleep before the end. Week-ends
visiting family in terraced houses, everyone crowded into front
rooms: our Jeannie, our Gracie, Mooch, Auntie Annie and her
Ian. The grown ups smoking as if their lives depended on it.
The girls hitting as hard as the boys. Auntie Alice's and Uncle
Eddie's: their two lads playing Rolling Stones' records upstairs,
home-brew in every cupboard, under the sink, in the glory-hole,
in the out-house, in the greenhouse, in the wardrobe

– come and have a taste of this lad – brown ale, bitter, brandy,
marrow rum. Auntie Alice dolloping out steaming dinners
that make your belly pop.

Being altar boys on Sunday mornings, then Checkley
for eggs and Cheshire Cheese from Len, his boots by the fire.
Him talking slow, Edie – his sister – busy at the stove. Home
in Henry the big black car, tinned tomatoes on toast
in front of the telly.

Family parties at the drop of a hat: party cans and egg-
rolls, trifles and crisps, hokey-cokeys and terrible dancing
to Status Quo, Auntie Lizzie's monologue. Us boys trying
for cool in market bought Ben Sherman's, brogues and two-
tone stay-press, reeking of Brüt; dancing with our cousins.
Aunt Jane a little merry lifting her skirt up her leg and shouting
look half a knicker. Three-card brag and poker for pennies.
Auntie Annie popping round next day on her moped for a chat.

Pate, we call him that, loves watching The Onedin Line,
building dreamboats in the garden, boozing in The Derby Arms
(a room behind the shop). Sometimes he takes us with him
and tells stories about Australia, where Bill was born, where he drove
oil tankers across the outback and didn't see another soul for days,
not even a mirage, fixed the pedal with a block of wood
and fell asleep at the wheel. Once he tried to tell us the facts of life,
but couldn't. He reads Exchange and Mart and JT Edson books:
A Town Called Yellow Dog, The Law of the Gun, A Horse Called Mogollon.
He lies under old cars in the new clothes we've bought
to smarten him up. He does what Besse tells him most of the time.

Besse rules us all with a tongue of iron, hands out advice,
dishes out justice, hands out love, fights for us all, watches the telly
with a silver cat on her lap, drinks ginger wine and smokes menthol
cigarettes, likes green and lets anyone in the house for a cup of tea.
One day I'll come home on leave and the taxi-driver will ask
what is that place?

32. MONEY TALKS

In 1940s Sheffield, my mum and her brothers grew up with little money and plenty of chores in a Methodist household with strict values. On one occasion they were told to take out the rubbish and sweep the yard. They set to it, whistling and bantering as they worked – and were amazed that my granddad gave them a shilling each when they finished. 'That's not for doing it,' he said. 'That's for whistling as you did it.'

That's a story about money. Oh, hang on – no it isn't. It tells us something about that family, about poverty, about their attitude to life after the war. The money – in this case, a specific coin which also places them in time – is only a hinge on which the story swings.

Think about *money*. You could mine the obvious references; a first pay slip, the cost of a car in 1978, a coin given to a beggar, the decision over whether to tip the hairdresser. By all means, have a vitriolic rant about what money means – 'I was led into money by the bitch business,' says C.H. Sisson in his poem 'Money'. But stories, like coinage, depreciate if handled carelessly. Don't debase the currency with nostalgia or vitriol. Work out what interests you about a particular image and pursue it so that it is about more than a coin or a car, or the predictable statement that monetary values change. Make money the focal point of a larger picture. Say something more than 'Ooh, folk today don't know the value of anything.' Or say that – but say it afresh.

Think of what money can buy – including simple pleasures like those enjoyed by Edna St. Vincent Millay, overleaf – and what it can't. There's also the coin that the tooth fairy left; the hoard of Roman coins reported in a newspaper; the settlement in your divorce. The fact that the poor often tip better than the rich. A sixpence in the Christmas pudding. The notes pinned to a Greek bride. Or imagine a different currency: how would it be if we paid for goods and services with paintings or, God help us, poetry?

Money talks, indeed. But listen carefully – it may not be saying what you thought.

EDNA ST. VINCENT MILLAY

Recuerdo

We were very tired, we were very merry—
We had gone back and forth all night on the ferry.
It was bare and bright, and smelled like a stable—
But we looked into a fire, we leaned across a table,
We lay on a hill-top underneath the moon;
And the whistles kept blowing, and the dawn came soon.

We were very tired, we were very merry—
We had gone back and forth all night on the ferry;
And you ate an apple, and I ate a pear,
From a dozen of each we had bought somewhere;
And the sky went wan, and the wind came cold,
And the sun rose dripping, a bucketful of gold.

We were very tired, we were very merry,
We had gone back and forth all night on the ferry.
We hailed, "Good morrow, mother!" to a shawl-covered head,
And bought a morning paper, which neither of us read;
And she wept, "God bless you!" for the apples and pears,
And we gave her all our money but our subway fares.

33. THE MACHINERY OF GRACE

Sometimes a poem has such grace and weight that you know it will survive far beyond the lifetime of its writer. 'Machines' by Michael Donaghy, opposite, is one such; you can hear him read it on the Poetry Archive website, for the full Donaghy experience.

Is this poem about bicycles? Is it hell as like. It's about love and balance, and plenty more besides. (The trick he pulls at the end, by the way – that elegant reversal of words – is called *chiasmus*.)

Look around you. Life is full of **machinery** – the computer, the iPod that goes running with you, the printer that hates you and chews up your essential document when you are in a rush. Some, like the kitchen clock or the immersion heater, are so familiar you barely see them. Some, like the Large Hadron Collider, are a source of awe or fear. A gun is a machine, but so is a pacemaker.

Perhaps your machine is an imagined one – a bullshit detector, an engine powered by daydreams or jealousy. Perhaps it's a historic one, like the first telephone. Whatever it is – and surely you know by now what I'm about to say – be *precise* in your choice. The machine itself is not the point. Use it as a prism for seeing beyond it. If changing a tyre for the first time or working out how to plumb in a washing machine were rites of passage for you, then the interesting thing is not the machine but its action on you. If the first compass or the enormous boring machines that cut the Channel Tunnel have some narrative appeal, then work out why and follow that thread.

Machines, after all, are not the important thing in life. Set your brain to work – and your heart too. These are the engines of poetry.

MICHAEL DONAGHY

Machines

Dearest, note how these two are alike:
This harpsicord pavane by Purcell
And the racer's twelve-speed bike.

The machinery of grace is always simple.
This chrome trapezoid, one wheel connected
To another of concentric gears,
Which Ptolemy dreamt of and Schwinn perfected,
Is gone. The cyclist, not the cycle, steers.
And in the playing, Purcell's chords are played away.

So this talk, or touch if I were there,
Should work its effortless gadgetry of love,
Like Dante's heaven, and melt into the air.

If it doesn't, of course, I've fallen. So much is chance,
So much agility, desire, and feverish care,
As bicyclists and harpsicordists prove

Who only by moving can balance,
Only by balancing move.

34. SO NEAR AND YET...

**'I nearly...sang 'Bat Out of Hell' to Bill Clinton and
Kevin Spacey but Jack Straw stopped me.'**
– Chris Meades, *Nearlyology*

Now there's a story. Oh, the things we *nearly* did. Think of
your own 'I nearly...' Not just something that didn't happen,
but something that very nearly did. That 'nearly' is your
subject. You nearly went to college, but got pregnant and
stayed at home. You nearly married that girl, and now she's
dead. You nearly took a job in Ipswich; nearly got a tattoo
but chickened out; nearly met John Lennon but went to the
snooker club instead. You nearly passed the 11+ and your
life was changed. You nearly failed the 11+ and wish you
had. You nearly nearly missed being there when someone
died, like Sharon Olds opposite.

What happened in that exact moment – were you
aware of your choice, or was it an innocent split second that
changed everything without you even grasping that you
had made a choice?

Nearly takes us to conditions of health and hope
– and not always our own. When Milton was almost blind,
when Newton was moments away from an understanding
of gravity – or when a child in the park is nearly able to
walk – what does the proximity to such a great event, the
anticipation of it, show us?

Don't think too hard about the word. Even a small
opportunity, whether missed or taken, will provide you
with your 'nearly'.

SHARON OLDS

The Race

When I got to the airport I rushed up to the desk,
bought a ticket, ten minutes later
they told me the flight was cancelled, the doctors
had said my father would not live through the night
and the flight was cancelled. A young man
with a dark brown moustache told me
another airline had a nonstop
leaving in seven minutes. See that
elevator over there, well go
down to the first floor, make a right, you'll
see a yellow bus, get off at the
second Pan Am terminal, I
ran, I who have no sense of direction
raced exactly where he'd told me, a fish
slipping upstream deftly against
the flow of the river. I jumped off that bus with those
bags I had thrown everything into
in five minutes, and ran, the bags
wagged me from side to side as if
to prove I was under the claims of the material,
I ran up to a man with a flower on his breast,
I who always go to the end of the line, I said
Help me. He looked at my ticket, he said
Make a left and then a right, go up the moving stairs and then
run. I lumbered up the moving stairs,
at the top I saw the corridor,
and then I took a deep breath, I said
goodbye to my body, goodbye to comfort,
I used my legs and heart as if I would

gladly use them up for this,
to touch him again in this life. I ran, and the
bags banged against me, wheeled and coursed
in skewed orbits, I have seen pictures of
women running, their belongings tied
in scarves grasped in their fists, I blessed my
long legs he gave me, my strong
heart I abandoned to its own purpose,
I ran to Gate 17 and they were
just lifting the thick white
lozenge of the door to fit it into
the socket of the plane. Like the one who is not
too rich, I turned sideways and
slipped through the needle's eye, and then
I walked down the aisle toward my father. The jet
was full, and people's hair was shining, they were
smiling, the interior of the plane was filled with a
mist of gold endorphin light,
I wept as people weep when they enter heaven,
in massive relief. We lifted up
gently from one tip of the continent
and did not stop until we set down lightly on the
other edge, I walked into his room
and watched his chest rise slowly
and sink again, all night
I watched him breathe.

35. RITES OF PASSAGE

'We need this thing. There's not one mineral in
Stonehenge that our blood can't also raise.'
– Albert Goldbarth, *Stonehenge*

What makes a *ritual*? A sense of occasion, marking a great
moment in life. A quality of closure or commencement, a
moment of witness. It can be rooted deep in the culture you
came from, like a bar mitzvah or baptism – or a wedding,
as in Maria Taylor's poem that follows. Even smaller rituals
can be hard to shake – crossing yourself when you enter a
church, singing a certain hymn as you do the washing up
– and even non-theists will remember a wedding, a funeral
or a moment of ceremony glimpsed whilst travelling.

Ritual can also mean the behavioural tic that
one *has* to do without knowing why. A football match or
the preparation of Sunday lunch has elements of ritual,
with its paraphernalia and patterns.

Invent a ritual for something which requires one. Be very
serious, or very silly. Something so universal has a lot to
offer. Devise a new ceremony for the opening of a Facebook
account or the final payment of your mortgage. Make a ritual
sacrifice to mark Getting Over Her, or a Blessing of the Car
Keys; have a cremation of desire or low self-esteem.

Take a vow to write a poem a week. Oh no, you did that
already.

Amen to that.

MARIA TAYLOR

Felling a Maiden

i.m. Maria Dimitri-Orthodoxou

And what did she bring to the altar?
A dowry sack of vowels, a grinding toothache
of consonants. In a few inky moments
she would no longer be foreign or hard to spell.

She was not from round here, torn
from fig and oleander, eucalyptus and sea,
though she didn't speak with a faraway voice
or make lace with her grandmother's needle.

After the wedding, I dismembered her.
I placed her in boxes, archived her into files;
her atoms looped among cobwebs and dust,
under attic beams. A suburban oubliette.

I swallowed the heart whole. She was gone.
The silence was everywhere.

36. SIGNED, SEALED, DELIVERED

**'I have copied it these thirteen years
waiting for the good bits – High King of the Roads,
are there any good bits in *The Grey Psalter of Antrim?*'**

That's Ian Duhig, writing as a scribe in his 'Margin Prayer from an Ancient Psalter'. Your own *important document* is probably more mundane than the psalter – perhaps your RSA Stage II Typing Certificate or your first driving license. Then again, it may be the adoption certificate that changed everything, your first house deeds or the unwanted Decree Absolute.

Remember the moment when it arrived. Root it in the physical world by telling us what it looked like. Use its impersonal language or its structure to inform your own piece.

Well, that's going to be a bundle of laughs isn't it? We don't actually want to read *about* a tax return, after all. A poem called 'Sod the Accounts, I am Going To The Pub' is far more interesting. If it's important, then what it stands for is important. In fact, Aracelis Girmay, overleaf, rejects dry documents altogether and looks to other priorities.

Or, go for a document that records someone else's life. You can happily lose days on lettersofnote.com, reading letters of note by public or private figures. Consider a legal document like Magna Carta or Domesday Book, or informal, ancient ones like the Vindolanda tablets (Google 'em). The word means 'handwritten' so tell us what it looks like, what the ink is made of.

Get it on paper. Beware sentimentality. Make it a document worth keeping.

ARACELIS GIRMAY

Elegy

*What to do with this knowledge
that our living is not guaranteed?*

Perhaps one day you touch the young branch
of something beautiful. & it grows & grows
despite your birthdays & the death certificate,
& it one day shades the heads of something beautiful
or makes itself useful to the nest. Walk out
of your house, then, believing in this.
Nothing else matters.

All above us is the touching
of strangers & parrots,
some of them human,
some of them not human.

Listen to me. I am telling you
a true thing. This is the only kingdom.
The kingdom of touching;
the touches of the disappearing, things.

37. WATER, WATER EVERYWHERE

'Thousands have lived without love, not one without water.'
– W.H. Auden

What took me so long to reach this subject? This week, we write about the metaphysical force that is *water*.

It's vast, in the oceans. It's tiny, in a single raindrop. It's familiar in the bedside glass, but powerful when imagined around the wreck of the Titanic. From giant squid to tadpoles, from diving in the sea to diving under the garden sprinkler, it saturates our frame of reference.

It's so ubiquitous, in fact, that you may find yourself drowning in ideas. You know what to do by now: get specific. Think about familiar landscapes – the seasides or streams you enjoy, the loch you fish in, that night of kayaking; your daily contact with water in the tap, the bath, the ritual of shaving. Think about episodes involving water; washing the dog, the laundry, the car or a moment when you nearly drowned. How to convey those sensations, the way the water catches light? Think about canals with their particular balance of the natural and artificial, their urban wildlife – I've indulged myself overleaf by using one of my own poems to illustrate the point.

Water may take you back to a basement flood or The Flood itself; to a vase of flowers or the icebergs of the Antarctic; to climate change and global water shortages, or right inside yourself to the personal reservoir that constitutes so much of your brain, your blood, your self. Go on a trip up the Amazon, down the Nile, around the Arctic Circle.

Follow, as water does, the path of least resistance.

Elementary, dear poet. Jump in.

Lifted

The land says – *come uphill*: and water says
I will. But take it slow.

A workman's ask and nothing fancy –
Will you? Here's an answer, engineered.

A leisurely machine, a box of oak and stone;
the mitred lock, the water's *YES*.

We're stopped. The bow bumps softly
at the bottom gate, and drifts.

All water wants, all water ever wants,
is to fall. So, we use the fall to lift us,

make of water its own tool, as simple
as a crowbar or a well-tied knot;

open up the paddles, let it dam and pucker,
lift and with it, lift us like a bride, a kite,

a wanted answer, breath no longer held
or like a boat. We're on our way

and rising. Water rushes in like fools;
these tonnages that slip across the cill,

all dirty-bottle green and gathering
into a giddy hurl then slower, slow until

it ends in glassy bulges, hints of aftermath:
a cool and thorough spending.

Wait, then, for the shudder in the gate,
the backward-drifting boat that tells you

there and here are level, an imbalance
righted. Ask of water; *help me rise*

and water says: *I will.*

38. WHATEVER IT IS, I'M AGAINST IT

…as Groucho Marx once sang. Now, ask yourself – what exactly are you *against*?

This isn't just something you dislike – chewing gum on pavements, reality TV – but something you really oppose. Something that offends you enough to send you to the barricades, or to take up arms, or write a stiff letter to the *Giggleswick Herald*.

There is a fine tradition of 'Against...' poems and like all traditions, it comes with pitfalls. Beware the ill-tempered rant, the immoderate polemic, the language of the pub bore. By all means rail against The Modern World or Bad Grammar: but in poetry as in personal speech, anger reduces an argument to easily-dismissed hyperbole. Keep your temper. State your case. Don't be a pub bore; be persuasive.

If you're stuck, think of something you're FOR, and look for its opposing number. If you love summer, write against winter. For and against. Yes and no. It's a simple, binary construct. Yes?

No. We are not simple, binary creatures: we are all about shades of maybe and perhaps. That may be where the interest of your poem lies. Roddy Lumsden claims to be 'Against Naturism', here, but it looks as though he's all for nakedness (and iambics too). Leave room for ambiguity.

Take a stand against lazy poetry.

RODDY LUMSDEN

Against Naturism

I realise it's not all salad sandwiches
at pinewood picnics, endless volleyball.
I've heard the argument that talk of shame
and how our forebears thought their bodies dirty;
how *we've all got one. Seen one, seen 'em all.*

But it's not for me, beneath my double load
of Calvinist and voyeuristic tendencies.
For me, I have to see the clothes come off:
the way a button's thumbed through cotton cloth –
a winning move in some exotic game

with no set rules but countless permutations –
or how a summer dress falls to the floor
with momentary mass and with a plash
that stirs us briefly as we ply our passion;
a hand pushed through the coldness of a zip,

three fingertips that follow down the spine
to where a clasp is neatly spun undone
amidkiss, by prime legerdemain
and who cares that it happens once in four
and never, never on the first undressing,

it must be better than a foreskin snagged
on gorse thorns or a cold, fat nipple jammed
in the scissor drawer, the bounty and the blessing,
the mystery of nakedness reduced
till on a par with go-go palaces

where goosebumped, grinding strippers strut their stuff
in the birthday clothes of backstreet empresses,
down on a par with the oncologist
who gropes for lumps, the night-morgue man who clips
his nails amongst the naked, bin-bagged stiffs.

So, stranger, what I want to say is this:
if you're to join me in a little sinning
(and this is my place up here on the right),
please understand I'd value some reluctance,
a cold-feet shiver, as in the beginning

when Eve discovered modesty and slipped
in and out of something comfortable.
For there are many ways to skin a cat,
but ours is human nature – things come off
so rarely. Come in. Let me take your coat.

39. YOUR SCHIEHALLION

Our next guest is Helen Mort, one of the Poetry Book Society's Next Generation Poets and winner of many awards for her work. Helen is deeply committed to her (and my) native land, the Peak District edge of Chesterfield and Sheffield. She engages with it not only by writing about its politics and cities, but also physically as a dedicated climber and runner. Helen writes:

'Oh, / There's a Schiehallion anywhere you go. / The thing is, climb it' – says Norman MacCaig in the following poem 'Landscape and I'. He's writing about the Scottish peak of that name, but I think he's writing about so much more – about mountains of the mind, about the way that places can seem very special and particular to us, but also so universal.

I remember climbing Schiehallion with my dad and his friend Dave when I was a teenager. We had to wait for ages at the top for Dave to catch up because he'd befriended a female hiker and was telling her all about the habits of black grouse. It was an unconventional chat-up line, I'll give him that. When we reached the top of the slope, I felt as if I was in the centre of Scotland and the world was made of nothing but mountains – the hills circled us like a moat.

I can remember every mountain I've climbed in better detail than I can remember what I did yesterday. When Norman MacCaig says 'there's a Schiehallion anywhere you go', I think part of what he means is that there are places of significance waiting for us everywhere, places that can imprint themselves on our memories.

There's another place that has done that for me, a kind of city Schiehallion. The place is Lowedges in Sheffield, only a ten minute drive from where I live, and my poem follows MacCaig's.

What's *your* Schiehallion? What memories do you have of being outdoors that you've never forgotten? It doesn't have to be a climb or an account of a great adventure. Your Schiehallion could be a corner of a garden, a swing in the park, a single, stolen flower. It could be an urban place instead of a rural one. But write about a place or a memory of being outdoors that means something to you.

Happy climbing.

NORMAN MacCAIG

Landscape and I

Landscape and I get on together well.
Though I'm the talkative one, still he can tell
His symptoms of being to me, the way a shell
Murmurs of oceans.

Loch Rannoch lapses dimpling in the sun.
Its hieroglyphs of light fade one by one
But re-create themselves, their message done,
For ever and ever.

That sprinkling lark jerked upward in the blue
Will daze to nowhere but leave himself in true
Translation – hear his song cascading through
His disappearance.

The hawk knows all about it, shaking there
An empty glove on steep chutes of the air
Till his yellow foot cramps on a squeal, to tear
Smooth fur, smooth feather.

This means, of course, Schiehallion in my mind
Is more than a mountain. In it he leaves behind
A meaning, an idea, like a hind
Couched in a corrie.

So then I'll woo the mountain till I know
The meaning of the meaning, no less. Oh,
There's a Schiehallion anywhere you go.
The thing is, climb it.

HELEN MORT

Lowedges

And if those doors to other worlds exist
you'll find them here: Lowedges, where the city
smooths its skirt down in the name of modesty,
picks up its jacket, calls it a night. Here, bichon frises
chase their tails all morning on the astroturf,

a biker lets go of his handlebars and doesn't fall,
a woman rolls the afternoon into a cigarette
and smokes it silently. Forget the Cornish sea,
the top of Nevis with its trapdoor light…
If you're to leave this world, you'll leave it here:
this salvaged Friday, shop lights dimmed. Look up –
how easily the rain bisects the sky.

40. HEADS AND SHOULDERS, KNEES AND TOES

Listen to your heart. There it is, bop bop bop. What if it went wrong? Now consider all those valiant body parts which have not gone wrong. Your strong legs, your unthanked eye. Maybe it's time to let them know how glad you are to have them.

Body parts are your subject. Think how much one organ (yes, including that one) can tell us about the whole person. It needn't be your own body part – a friend's brain, as she recovers from surgery; the surgeon's hand or van Gogh's severed ear. Daniel Sluman's moving poem, opposite, comes from his experience of losing a leg as a child.

Be a hypochondriac and think, for once, about all the things you try not to think about. Reflect on the subtleties of the brain, the tongue, the inner ear. Do some homework to find out why we still have an appendix, since it does nothing. And does the clitoris or the root canal really extend that far? Ah well, that would explain it.

This is not about The Body in general. That way lies vagueness, and in vagueness lies mediocrity. So this week is all about that one specific part of the body. Write an ode to it, celebrate or chastise it; or harness it, as Elizabeth I did overleaf, to comment on something less corporeal.

Get your teeth into it. Put your back into it. You get the idea.

DANIEL SLUMAN

in dreams

I have two legs   my mother stays
& childhood is a single house

a bursting fridge with music

crashing through the hall
the record-player's needle

is the only one that will tear

into my life   I am a thing
worth loving   & I love

in controlled explosions

nobody is hurt   the script
hacked into my skin with a knife

un-picks itself like a thread

& ambulances only ever pass
my tempered heart ticks

in line with everyone else's

with a gin in my hand I drink
myself to perfection each night

QUEEN ELIZABETH I

Written in her French Psalter

No crooked leg, no bleared eye,
No part deformed out of kind,
Nor yet so ugly half can be
As is the inward suspicious mind.

PETER CARPENTER

Gift

after a line by Mandelstam

A body. My very own possession –
what am I to make of you?
Devoted life-partner, let me know
who to thank. Involuntary father

confessor to my thousand secrets –
the crop circles of eczema,
the crisis of thinning hair –
comforter through night terrors,

you give me the freedom
to hold up a finger, thus,

and say I touch the sky.

41. FOOD FOR THOUGHT

'One cannot think well, love well, sleep well, if one has not dined well.' – Virginia Woolf

'There are people in the world so hungry, that God cannot appear to them except in the form of bread.'
– Mahatma Gandhi

Forty prompts later, we get around to this subject. How peculiar. After all, *food* is an obvious theme, right?

Ah, but obvious subjects come with deep pitfalls. In this case it's nostalgia, which is a kind of poetic comfort eating. We probably don't need a long wistful poem about how the taste of your mother's stew can send you back to 1988. (Unless, of course, we do. Your poem, your rules. But it had better be *damn* good stew).

Goodness knows, you have the raw material. After all, you have eaten every day of your life and usually more than once; sometimes barely noticing your hurried breakfast, sometimes taking time to savour a snack. Food is a sacrament, a kind of foreplay, a chore, a cultural identifier. So basic a need, so often met, opens up a huge hinterland of association and memory. Write a poem as a recipe – or a recipe as a poem, as Sydney Smith did in the eighteenth century, in the poem that follows.

As at the best dinner party, food is on the table only as the catalyst for conversation. If avocados remind you of that holiday in Mexico, then away you go. If Oxo cubes dissolved in boiling water kept you alive during a childhood illness, then your subject is not Oxo cubes but weakness, mortality, a mother's love.

Whet our appetites. Leave us hungry for more.

SYDNEY SMITH

A Recipe for Salad

Two boiled potatoes strained through a kitchen sieve,
Softness and smoothness to the salad give;
Of mordant mustard take a single spoon,
Distrust the condiment that bites too soon!
Yet deem it not, thou man of taste, a fault
To add a double quantity of salt.
Four times the spoon with oil of Lucca crown,
And twice with vinegar procured from town;
True taste requires it and your poet begs
The pounded yellow of two well-boiled eggs.
Let onion's atoms lurk within the bowl
And, scarce suspected, animate the whole,
And lastly in the flavoured compound toss
A magic spoonful of anchovy sauce.
Oh, great and glorious! Oh, herbaceous meat!
'Twould tempt the dying Anchorite to eat,
Back to the world he'd turn his weary soul
And plunge his fingers in the salad bowl.

42. WITH A SONG IN YOUR HEART

Song is our subject this week. Song goes from the ear straight to the heart – a primitive, sophisticated, tribal, private, simple and complex thing. For our purposes, there are at least three ways of tackling it.

1. Write about the *act* of singing. A family rendition of Happy Birthday, a drunken get-together.... Perhaps you joined the rugby club in a rousing version of Eskimo Nell. Maybe your grandmother was a Methodist with hymns hard-wired into her bones. Singing can also be a momentary relief from suffering, as in Siegfried Sassoon's famous 'Everyone Sang'.

2. Write the song itself. Yours may be a battle song, a song of praise for your new vacuum cleaner or an exhortation to a friend to come through a hard time. It can be an anthem like '(Sing if You're) Glad to be Gay', or a moment of perfect silliness like Edwin Morgan's 'Loch Ness Monster's Song' (find it on the excellent website of the Scottish Poetry Library).

3. Write about a song that has meaning for you. Beware: this approach in particular is a minefield, full of sentimental tosh. 'Do you remember that fantastic moment at the Bob Dylan concert when we all sang together...?' The reader wasn't there, so make it matter to reader as well as writer.

Off you go, with a pen in your hand and a song in your heart.

KEI MILLER

Unsung

There should be a song for the man who does not sing
himself – who has lifted a woman from her bed to a wheelchair
each morning, and from a wheelchair to her bed each night;
a song for the man recognized by all the pharmacists, because
each day he has joined a line, inched forward with a prescription
for his ailing wife; there should be a song for this man
who has not sung himself; he is father to an unmarried son
and will one day witness the end of his name; still he has refused
to pass down shame to his boy. There should be a song
for the man whose life has not been the stuff of ballads
but has lived each day in incredible and untrumpeted ways.
There should be a song for my father.

43. THE UNSEEN

'"All right," said the Cat; and this time it vanished quite slowly, beginning with the end of the tail, and ending with the grin, which remained some time after the rest of it had gone.' – Lewis Carroll, *Alice in Wonderland*

Poets, I hereby give you license to write about *the unseen*. But read on, Macduff.

I *don't* mean God, Time, the ghost in the upstairs bedroom or anything so abstract. That way lies madness, hyperbole and Very Bad Poetry for the most part. I mean those physical things that we know to exist, but which we can't see with the naked eye.

Under this heading would come microbes, the fish in the local canal or the bicycle, ditto; a group of people with whom you feel kinship though you don't know them, such as fellow joggers. The rivers underneath our cities, as in U.A. Fanthorpe's poem overleaf. The cities that lie beneath our fields. The ever more distant boundary of the universe or, somewhere spinning within it, the Voyager satellite with its cargo of recorded sound.

Give a moment's thought to the unseen neighbour eating Weetabix (or worshipping Satan) as you eat your boiled egg on the other side of the wall, or the skylark singing too high to spot. If you know it exists, but you can't see it, then it's a possible subject. The things you can't see are often more interesting than the things you can.

It's perfectly simple. All you have to do is pick a thing you can't see and look at it very closely. Then show us what it looks like.

See?

U.A. FANTHORPE

Rising Damp

At our feet they lie low,
The little fervent underground
Rivers of London

Effra, Graveney, Falcon, Quaggy,
Wandle, Walbrook, Tyburn, Fleet

Whose names are disfigured,
Frayed, effaced.

There are the Magogs that chewed the clay
To the basin that London nestles in.
These are the currents that chiselled the city,
That washed the clothes and turned the mills,
Where children drank and salmon swam
And wells were holy.

They have gone under.
Boxed, like the magician's assistant.
Buried alive in earth.
Forgotten, like the dead.

They return spectrally after heavy rain,
Confounding suburban gardens. They inflitrate
Chronic bronchitis statistics. A silken
Slur haunts dwellings by shrouded
Watercourses, and is taken
For the footing of the dead.

Being of our world, they will return
(Westbourne, caged at Sloane Square,
Will jack from his box),
Will deluge cellars, detonate manholes,
Plant effluent on our faces,
Sink the city.

Effra, Graveney, Falcon, Quaggy,
Wandle, Walbrook, Tyburn, Fleet

It is the other rivers that lie
Lower, that touch us only in dreams
That never surface. We feel their tug
As a dowser's rod bends to the surface below

Phlegethon, Acheron, Lethe, Styx.

44. MOVING PICTURES

This prompt, more than any other, was difficult to convert from the blog where 52 began, because of its many useful links to films and other images. Read it carefully and remember that you can use any film of your own choosing. It comes from Rachael Boast, winner of multiple prizes including the Forward First Collection Prize. Often described as a modern metaphysical poet, she lives in Bristol.

'Moving images' is a phrase that evokes several interpretations. As a noun, we immediately think about the genre of film, but could also interpret this phrase as any images that are perceived to be moving, as opposed to fixed in one place. As a verb, it could be understood as the imaginative act of moving an image from one place to another – in a sense, this is what the imagination does when at work on poetry. An image in a poem can 'move' from having one association to having another and may also move from meaning to meaning, depending on the active effects of other images in a poem.

Write *a poem about a film* – ideally one that has literature, or a literary figure, as subject or creator. This is an act of ekphrasis, which simply means 'art about art'. For our purposes, it means an attempt to expand the meaning or significance of a film through the heightened use of language particular to poetry – and in so doing, bring the moving image alive with a new intelligence. Examples are the films of Andre Tarkovsky (especially *Mirror* which incorporates poems composed and read by his father Arseny) or *Pandaemonium*, Julien Temple's film on Coleridge and Wordsworth.

This is also a good excuse to watch the films of Jean Cocteau who saw film, as well as drawing and painting for that matter, as a form of moving poetry (*Heurtebise* is both the subject of a poem, and a film character). My own second collection, *Pilgrim's Flower,* began and ended with ekphrastic poems based on Cocteau's *La Belle et la Bête* and *Le Sang d'un Poète,* respectively.

Written your film poem? Next: ask yourself what would your poem look like, as a film?

45. THE UNCERTAINTY PRINCIPLE

In reading the many poems I used for this book, very few struck me as forcefully as the one opposite, by Edwin Bok Lee. Read every last word of it, and read it again. You may also call to mind Rudyard Kipling's anthemic poem 'If' – 'If you can keep your head, when all about you are losing theirs....'

Both poems, though very different, operate on the same principle. Everything hangs on the first word – **IF**. The outcome – making up your mind in a split second whether to shoot your pursuers, or conducting yourself through life as a man apparently should – depends on the choice which you, the reader, make in response to that uncertainty posed by the writer. The writer asks a question – the reader answers it.

That little word is the first word of your poem. Whatever follows it, your piece must begin with If.

Where do you go after that? Address the big ifs – if there is life after death, "if the Son shall set you free...." or consider those sliding-door moments when you took one path, and wonder what might have happened if you had taken the other. If I had bought that red sports car/ taken heroin when offered/ not taken heroin when offered – how would my life have been different?

Poetry is about extracting maximum value from each word, even the tiny ones. The two letters of 'if' stand for all kinds of uncertainty. Uncertainty is what will drive your reader on through the poem, until you deliver some kind of certainty.

If, of course, you choose to.

ED BOK LEE

If In America

Hmong Hunter Charged with 6 Murders
Is Said to Be a Shaman —NEW YORK TIMES

If a tree falls in a forest,
does it make a sound?

If a rifle fires a shot in the woods,
whose body first hits the ground?

If a group of angry hunters
surrounds, curses at, and accosts you
for wandering onto their land

If you apologize for being lost,
inform you saw no posted signs, swallow
their chinks this and gooks taking over that;
are walking away over mud and fallen leaves when a loud
crack far behind you kicks up black earth

If your father was conscripted to fight
on the side of the United States
for the CIA during the war in Vietnam

If he, your mother, you—the oldest son—
and all your younger siblings were later abandoned
in the hills of Laos as targets for genocide by the Viet Cong

If after five years in a Thai refugee camp,
you come to this land as a teen, a casualty
of history and time, then receive three years
of training to become a sharpshooter
in the U.S. military

If you spent your adolescence watching blacks,
Asians, Latinos, and whites watching one
another watch each other for weakness and flaws

If, after this first blast, you wheel
around in a bright orange vest; glimpse
in that split second an angry, possibly
inebriated man lowering *or* resighting his rifle

If, in that icy moment, you recall
the Native friend you used to collect cans with;
once watched his three-hundred-pound father
unload himself from a Chevy Impala and chase
the boy down University with a ball-peen hammer

If, of your own children, your quietest
son lately lacks the wherewithal at school
to defend himself; and your oldest daughter
has always been for some inexplicable reason
ashamed of you

If hunting for you is not just a sport;
never a time to drink beers
with friends in a cabin, but rather
is a factor in considering your family's winter protein
     consumption

If you believe in God, but not the good in everyone

If you hate to think about this shit, because
why the fuck is it always on you
to preprove your loyalty and innocence?

If—frightened for your life and
the livelihood of your immediate and extended
family—in that split second, you reel
and train your own gun back at the far face
of that vapory barrel now aiming at your own

If, yes, you are sometimes angry and so look forward
to escaping your truck driver's life on certain
designated dates, on certain designated
lands, not always clearly demarcated, but always clearly stolen
from the ancestors of fat drunk red men
so confused they chase their own firey songs
in the form of their sons

Stolen from generations of skewed black backs,
hunched your whole life on street corners laughing
and picking their bones

Stolen from the paychecks of your brown coworker
social security ghosts

Stolen like your own people
from mountains in one land
only to be resettled and resented here
in projects and tenements

If you barely finished high school, but you know
from all you've ever seen of this system
Might Makes Right,
and excuses, treaties, and cover-ups
appear the only true code inscribed on most white men's
      souls

If, after such slurs, pushes, and threats in these woods
it is now also on you to assess
if that far rifle still locked on your face
just issued a mistake, a warning
shot, or murderous attempt—

                              and the answer is:
your military muscle fibers
act

If you then spot three four five six seven? other
hunters now scattering for their ATVs
and, of course—if a gook,
don't be a dumb one—
scattering now also for their weapons

If you are alone in this land,
on foot, in miles of coming snow, wind, and branches
and don't even know
in which direction you'd run

If from birth you've seen
what men with guns, knives,
and bombs are capable of doing
for reasons you never wanted to understand

If in this very same county's court of all-white
witnesses, counsel, judge, and jurors
it will forever be your word against theirs
because there was no forensic testimony
over who shot first

If, yes, sometimes you can hear voices,
not because you're insane, but
in your culture
you are a shaman, a spiritual healer,

though in this very different land
of goods and fears, your only true worth
seems to be as a delivery man and soldier

If, upon that first fateful exchange in these woods,
your instinct, pushing pin to
balloon, were to tell you it's now
either you and your fatherless family of fourteen,
or *all* of them

Would *you* set your rifle down;
hope the right, the decent,
the fair thing on this buried American soil
will happen?

Or would you stay low,
one knee cold, and do
precisely as your whole life
and history have trained?

And if you did,
would anyone even care
what really happened

that afternoon
eight bodies plummeted
to earth like deer?

46. SPOKEN WORD

'We have a very equal relationship. She does all the cooking, I do all the welding.'

That sentence, which I overheard recently on a bus, sends me back to a favourite theme – **the overheard**. A poet's job is to pay attention. Look. Listen. Learn. So, go forth and eavesdrop: at the bus stop, in the newsagent or at the school gate. Overheard words give you a flavour of someone else's life.

Incorporate a single overheard phrase in your poem. Or make the whole poem reported speech – invent some, if necessary. It need not be pleasant – it might be contemptuous, embarrassing. Just because your poem starts from an overhearing, it doesn't have to start *with* an overhearing. Sometimes the strongest telling is the wrong way round, so that we arrive at the spoken phrase last.

This prompt gives you license to sit in a coffee shop and listen. Pay attention, as a writer always should, to what is said at the service station, the supermarket, the hotel reception desk. If you are housebound then use the radio, but make sure that your 'overheard' phrase is spontaneous, and not scripted, speech – a phone-in or interview is a good source.

Much of what you hear will be banal and uninteresting, but even *Good morning Mr Jones* has potential. Has that phrase been uttered twenty times this month with a cheery face, but with a growing sense of hatred/ unrequited love/ bitterness? Tell that person's imagined story – or remember someone saying something similar to you. It can even be a historic overhearing – a family argument, a phone call you wish you hadn't heard – but an overhearing, not something said directly to you.

Cheers, big ears. Listen up.

CLAIRE CROWTHER

Heritage

'*Get That Tiger* isn't a hymn,' my mother
muttered under the muttering of the Mass.

Later, her Costa face tint showed up odd
against the plain Tudor Catholic walls.

The priests' hole behind a bookshelf was labelled
a library. 'Can't have had much learning,'

a blonde boy said. 'Douai,' said Father Thomas.
I scrambled down a ladder. At the bottom, soil.

'Not much they'd be doing here,' said Phyllis,
'but praying.' It isn't a hymn. Monks were dressed

as celebrities. We photographed them, laughing
by the moat. 'They dress up for visitors,'

Big Nurnie said. 'Cassocks.' My mother slapped
her sandwich down on her missal. My son kept on

about the ways they executed priests.
'Who is this *they*?' I asked. It isn't a hymn.

There comes a time when you switch off from listening
and lose someone. I traced her back to the hole.

O Mary, Mother of God, you get that tiger,
full of grace, and you sing her to us.

47. LEARNING YOUR LESSON

'The best thing for being sad,' replied Merlyn,
beginning to puff and blow, 'is to learn something. That
is the only thing that never fails.'
– T.H. White, *The Once and Future King*

He's right, of course. The passage, and the book from which that quote comes are worth reading and re-reading. It's poetic enough to maybe count as a prose poem, if you believe in that sort of thing. This prompt is a short one, because it's self-explanatory: *what have you learned?*

What did you learn at school or at university – was it any use? Then again, what did you learn during ten years of domestic abuse, or thirty years of working for the civil service? If you were to title your poem 'Things X Taught Me' then what is X – a dog, a river, Wigan Casino, alcohol, the Incredible Hulk? You might list the things you learned at university, or wonder as Peter Carpenter does opposite what others learned, or make an oblique study of, for instance, The Way I Learned to Write.

Booby trap alert: beware sentimentality, pomposity, mawkishness, a Hallmark-card poem wistfully telling us that you have learned How To Be Kind or Not to Interfere. The solution: avoid abstracts ruthlessly – wisdom, pain, joy etc. Keep it concrete. Illustrate every lesson with the five senses. Resist the urge to say in those fatal last two lines – *and so I learned that....* It should be clear by then.

Be brave or breezy, but dig deep. Make this one count; you may even learn something in the process.

Keith Standing

Field mushroom ears. Monday's callus of snot
or mashed potato still there on frayed Aertex collar come Friday.
John Lennon specs bleared by fingerprints, ice-rink scoured;
basin crewcut, involuntary half-grin, right arm braced permanently
in the air. Class fall guy, back-up anarchist when General Science
with Doc Death had passed its sell-by date.

'Sir, sir, I've swallowed some copper sulphate, sir.'

A frothy lisp of ocean-blue cola. Epsom District. Sirens, the works.

You grew on us. A trouper. For P.E. repeated offence:
coal-dust socks, no House vest. Punishment: in sheeting rain
to pick flints off terraced pitches down at Priest Hill. Undaunted,
you deliver them in a sack to Norris's desk like Millet's Sower
in steamed-over cartoon specs. Every day, arm aloft, the grin.
'Erm someone else… no, not you, Standing.'

'Sir, sir, I've got a rubber stuck up my nose, sir.'

But here's a question for you, Keith – how did it go? Not
the extraction of that tough khaki-green lozenge, but all those
after school activities – your late teens, employment, raising
a family, bank statements, the long haul, your life?

You can put your hand down now.

48. MACARONI, NO CHEESE

Our final guest, Philip Gross, is one of our most versatile and exploratory poets. He loves to play with language, its possibilities and limitations. Philip often works with other artists, or revives archaic forms like the *glosa*, to enrich the ground from which we dig our poems. Philip's prompt is more technical than most in this book but it would work with a dialect, baby talk or any kind of jargon. Philip writes:

Macaronic verse is poetry in which two languages co-exist, often in alternating form, so that one implicitly comments on the other. Historically, this has sometimes been used for irony or protest; this poem from fourteenth-century England alternates lines of Middle English with medieval Latin – roughly, the language of the common people set against the language of power in that time. (The translation below is very rough!)

> The taxe hath tened vs alle,
> *Probat hoc mors tot validorum*
> The Kyng þereof had small
> *ffuit in minibus cupidorum*
> yt had ful hard hansell,
> *dans causam fine dolorum;*
> vengeaunce nedes most fall,
> *propter peccata malorum*

> The tax has ruined us all
> *It proves the death of all worthy men*
> The king has small gain from it
> *It falls into the hands of the greedy*

It was a token of ill fortune
And the cause of endless woes
Vengeance certainly must fall
On account of the evil man's sins

[From the Digby collection (196) in the Bodleian Library, Oxford]

Incidentally this can be a brilliant discipline for the ear: asking one language to rhyme with another makes us very aware of the different, maybe never quite compatible, sound qualities of each. Macaronic verse can be used to explore more sensitive emotions too – the poem below may make a real French speaker wince, but the distance and sound-slippage between the languages is meant to be part of the point.

L'exilé qui a perdu sa langue
Turns startled by the…. is it song?
des martinets arrives d'autrefois
or is it weeping? They have come too far.
L'étranger a oublié son nom
where he was going to, or coming from
mais ces oiseaux ont traversé le ciel,
their cries as wordless as a tolling bell.
Les mots étaient trop lourds, trop difficiles.
Without them we can soar and screech and wheel.
Ils ne restent jamais, jamais sur le terre,
its history, its logic, waiting there.
Même s'ils n'ont plus rien a dire
that *nothing* strikes him now, like fear.

The French lines above translate a little like this: The exile who has lost his language/ The swift arriving from long ago / The stranger has forgotten his name / but those birds have

153

crossed the sky / words were too heavy, too difficult/ they
never, never rest on the earth / although they have nothing
more to say.

*Please note, you do not need to possess two language to write
macaronically.* Not only are there dialects and accents within
English, there are many *registers* of language – the legal, say,
or the bureaucratic, the languages of medicine or therapy
or politics, or of any occupational sub-culture; each has its
own tone and vocabulary, its own resident references and
clichés.

If you feel moved to try a bilingual piece, of course, do...
but for the purposes of this exercise, try a macaronic poem
in two registers of English. How you define those registers,
and even the use of rhyme or not, is up to you. The main
thing is to hear the difference between them, and make
creative use of it.

49. EVERYTHING IS ILLUMINATED

Is it dark outside, or light as you read this? Think about *light*.

Consider daylight first. This morning, the quality and sheer *quantity* of sunlight in my living room was astonishing. And now that it's dark... but it isn't, of course. There are still many kinds of light to see. There's an almost-full moon, giving off a cold sheen. The stars each have a different quality of luminescence – some rose-pink, some white. Occasionally a plane passes over with its tail lights flashing slowly. In my living room the fire gives out a warm glow which would devour everything if released.

For photographers or thieves, light means exposure. In the art of Vermeer or Cranach it can be moving and subtle. Think of candlelight, moonlight, flash bulbs, fireballs.

When the lights go out, what happens in the dark? In the darkroom, the bedroom, the coffin, in the cave when your torch gives out? When it's dark here, what's happening on the other side of the world? What is it like to lose light – to go blind, or to enter the extreme Arctic winter, knowing that dawn that won't come for six months? Read Donne's famous, complicated poem below – a lament written after the death of his wife. It's a cry of despair and loss in the longest night of the year.

Illuminating, no?

JOHN DONNE

A Nocturnal upon St Lucy's Day

Being the shortest day of the year

'Tis the year's midnight, and it is the day's,
Lucy's, who scarce seven hours herself unmasks;
     The sun is spent, and now his flasks
     Send forth light squibs, no constant rays;
       The world's whole sap is sunk;
The general balm th' hydroptic earth hath drunk,
Whither, as to the bed's feet, life is shrunk,
Dead and interr'd; yet all these seem to laugh,
Compar'd with me, who am their epitaph.

Study me then, you who shall lovers be
At the next world, that is, at the next spring;
     For I am every dead thing,
     In whom Love wrought new alchemy.
       For his art did express
A quintessence even from nothingness,
From dull privations, and lean emptiness;
He ruin'd me, and I am re-begot
Of absence, darkness, death: things which are not.

All others, from all things, draw all that's good,
Life, soul, form, spirit, whence they being have;
     I, by Love's limbec, am the grave
     Of all that's nothing. Oft a flood
       Have we two wept, and so
Drown'd the whole world, us two; oft did we grow
To be two chaoses, when we did show
Care to aught else; and often absences
Withdrew our souls, and made us carcasses.

But I am by her death (which word wrongs her)
Of the first nothing the elixir grown;
    Were I a man, that I were one
    I needs must know; I should prefer,
        If I were any beast,
Some ends, some means; yea plants, yea stones detest,
And love; all, all some properties invest;
If I an ordinary nothing were,
As shadow, a light and body must be here.

But I am none; nor will my sun renew.
You lovers, for whose sake the lesser sun
    At this time to the Goat is run
    To fetch new lust, and give it you,
        Enjoy your summer all;
Since she enjoys her long night's festival,
Let me prepare towards her, and let me call
This hour her vigil, and her eve, since this
Both the year's, and the day's deep midnight is.

50 – PULLING PUNCHES

'To paraphrase several sages: Nobody can think and hit someone at the same time.' – Susan Sontag

'People sleep peaceably in their beds at night only because rough men stand ready to do violence on their behalf.' – George Orwell

Brace yourself. Your theme this week is *violence*.

I mean an incident of personal violence. It may have happened to you – a parent smacking you, a racist attack, or it may be only the aftermath that you witnessed. You may have contemplated violence yourself, or acted on it. Look back at Week 10 and William Letford's headbutt, and at David Morley's brutal poem, 'Three', which follows here.

In poetry, comfort is a kind of cowardice, so try to confront yourself. Have you ever *enjoyed* violence – in a playground fight, an act of spite or revenge, at a boxing match or hearing of the death of a tyrant? Did you witness a fight and do nothing? Dig deep. There may be shame in the memory.

There's a powerful trick for tackling the dark stuff in our lives; change your viewpoint. If this is a tale of *you* doing something awful, change it to the third person. If it's 's/he' doing it, that makes it easier to tell. By the same token, if it's a story of you being attacked, try writing as the attacker. It will be ugly; but then it should be. And resist, resist, resist those damn abstracts. Don't say 'pain' or 'shock' or 'terror' –show us how it physically looks and smells – the sound of a punch, the way a person flinches or squares up. Show the readers an actual bruise, and trust them to deduce the deeper wounds.

And yet, there is good in the world. Go forth. Pull no punches.

DAVID MORLEY

Three

I am trying to behave but my father
has a fist crammed with kitchen knives
like a brilliant new hand, and the rest
of us in the house are suddenly not alive.
One of us is guilty of the crime of two biscuits.
One of us has taken biscuits without permission
so all are condemned and have earned his lesson
which is to cower in the bedroom's corner
without cover while he slices our arteries open
in the air between us. His house is his abattoir.
His home is lit with hooks and steel hands.
We are not alive as he bars the bedroom door.

The morning is ordinary because I am three.
My brother unwinds a lace from his shoe.
He works its little rope across the hearth
until it makes a dripping strip of light and flame
that he slips slowly on the back of my hand.
I am trying to behave as though this never happened,
keeping my scorched hand below the tablecloth
while my father, sick with guilt, serves us soup.
My brother knows I can soak up his secrets.
My left fingers misbehave and my father
forces the hand. Sered sores. A veal of veins.
My brother at this time is being flung into a wall
and all I am thinking is that I do not like oxtail.

I do not like the blood thirst of what I can hear
through the floor of my bedroom as my father
flies off his handle again, but this is a real handle
that he's handling as a weapon, and the sitting room
is being smashed and smashed and smashed to death.
Better the mirrors, I think, than my mother.
But he's upstairs by now, kicking his way up
and dread is draining through that black wall
but the wall doesn't shelter, not when there's a door
to be hurled off its hinges like it was never there,
him yanking me by my cock to his yelling height
before dropping me down a well in that dark room.
His face swells to fill the door as he finds his range.

51.   YEAR OF THE GOAT

G.K. Chesterton famously said, 'The poets have been mysteriously silent on the subject of cheese'. There's always *some* fresh angle on the world. Let's look at how a single, unexpected word can give us access to new things.

It isn't cheese – that would be silly. It's **goat**.

Stop tittering at the back. That word will serve as well as any other, to illustrate that any subject will do as a starting point for a poem. Goats are real, yet somehow dreamlike, as in Elizabeth Bishop's famous poem 'Crusoe in England'. They have a powerful otherness that takes the reader elsewhere, but they are also comical. They bring a rich hinterland of myth, as in Elizabeth Barrett Browning's poem which follows.

If you have a goat in your life or can remember one – from childhood, from the Pyrenees, from an experience of goat curry, or being a Capricorn, or seeing the constellation of that name – then so much the better. If you don't, then you will have to make it up. Write freely and fabulously, but just make sure there is a goat in it somewhere; a real one, an ornament, a toy. Dig deep, as you always have, and see if something unusual comes of your caprine subconscious.

Goats? Seriously? Yes. No kidding.

ELIZABETH BARRETT BROWNING

A Musical Instrument

I.

What was he doing, the great god Pan,
  Down in the reeds by the river ?
Spreading ruin and scattering ban,
Splashing and paddling with hoofs of a goat,
And breaking the golden lilies afloat
  With the dragon-fly on the river.

II.

He tore out a reed, the great god Pan,
  From the deep cool bed of the river :
The limpid water turbidly ran,
And the broken lilies a-dying lay,
And the dragon-fly had fled away,
  Ere he brought it out of the river.

III.

High on the shore sate the great god Pan,
  While turbidly flowed the river ;
And hacked and hewed as a great god can,
With his hard bleak steel at the patient reed,
Till there was not a sign of a leaf indeed
  To prove it fresh from the river.

IV.

He cut it short, did the great god Pan,
  (How tall it stood in the river !)
Then drew the pith, like the heart of a man,
Steadily from the outside ring,
And notched the poor dry empty thing
  In holes, as he sate by the river.

V.

This is the way,' laughed the great god Pan,
   Laughed while he sate by the river,)
The only way, since gods began
To make sweet music, they could succeed.'
Then, dropping his mouth to a hole in the reed,
   He blew in power by the river.

VI.

Sweet, sweet, sweet, O Pan !
   Piercing sweet by the river !
Blinding sweet, O great god Pan !
The sun on the hill forgot to die,
And the lilies revived, and the dragon-fly
   Came back to dream on the river.

VII.

Yet half a beast is the great god Pan,
   To laugh as he sits by the river,
Making a poet out of a man :
The true gods sigh for the cost and pain, —
For the reed which grows nevermore again
   As a reed with the reeds in the river.

52. A VALEDICTION: FORBIDDING MOURNING

'Write a poem a week. Start now. Keep going.'

If you have been writing a poem a week, then you're approaching the end of your year. And if this book has been any kind of success, it will have shown you that you can write about anything, from eyeballs to small change. You don't *need* a prompt: just look at the world around you. The raw material is everywhere – but the subject is always the same. The subject is *you*; or at least your world view, which you cannot escape. Your taste for avocado, your hatred of jazz, your horror at the latest US school massacre, your shiny new shoes or tired old feet.

    The value of poetry is surely to share experience, precisely and with impact, so that reader and writer can connect. Poetry is the opposite of small talk. It is communication, on the level of emotion. A poet says *I think the world is like this. Is it like this for you?* and with any luck the reader says *Why, yes. I recognise that.* Your job as a poet is to be wholly human, alive to the world around you, and to share your findings.

Our first prompt was a rip-roaring declaration of energy and appetite. The last is, of course, a leave-taking – but one in which sadness is prohibited. Taking your cue from the brilliant metaphysical poet John Donne, overleaf, your mission is to write *A Valediction: Forbidding Mourning.*

    A valediction is simply a poem of goodbye. It implies a parting, a leaving behind. But yours will turn an ending into a triumph.

Now, John Donne is many things but 'childishly easy to understand' is not one of them. 'Metaphysical' is after all Greek for 'much cleverer than you'. If you find this poem a bit of a brain-teaser, you are not alone. Read it again until your head hurts, which it will do. Basically he's saying: *I'll be back. We can't be separated even by death, because we're always together.*

What do you want to say goodbye to? Perhaps to an old habit, an old house. Imagine a historic goodbye – read 'Gloriana Dying' on the poetryarchive.org to find Elizabeth I, splendidly haughty on her deathbed. Imagine Yuri Gagarin saying goodbye to the much-loved Earth and wondering what space will bring. Goodbye to parents, as you leave for university – goodbye to a marriage which, though it's over, has taught you things you both needed to learn. Goodbye to the family as they leave on Boxing Day, allowing you to reclaim the house. Goodbye to 52, and hello to whatever comes next. After all, a farewell to what came before can become a declaration of fresh discovery – as in Keats' following poem.

The 52 project which led to this book spawned thousands of poems. Some have been published in journals and have won big competitions, or become the kernel of new books. If that's what you're looking for, then I wish you luck. But the most important measure of success – the only one that counts – is that you sit down to write something, and you make it as good as you can. If you've missed a week here and there – or if you've missed months and months – don't beat yourself up. Just keep writing, when you can. For now, let's have a valediction without mournfulness.

Say goodbye with joy.
And then? KEEP GOING.

JOHN DONNE

A Valediction: Forbidding Mourning

As virtuous men pass mildly away,
  And whisper to their souls to go,
Whilst some of their sad friends do say
  The breath goes now, and some say, No:

So let us melt, and make no noise,
  No tear-floods, nor sigh-tempests move;
'Twere profanation of our joys
  To tell the laity our love.

Moving of th' earth brings harms and fears,
  Men reckon what it did, and meant;
But trepidation of the spheres,
  Though greater far, is innocent.

Dull sublunary lovers' love
  (Whose soul is sense) cannot admit
Absence, because it doth remove
  Those things which elemented it.

But we by a love so much refined,
  That our selves know not what it is,
Inter-assured of the mind,
  Care less, eyes, lips, and hands to miss.

Our two souls therefore, which are one,
  Though I must go, endure not yet
A breach, but an expansion,
  Like gold to airy thinness beat.

If they be two, they are two so
  As stiff twin compasses are two;
Thy soul, the fixed foot, makes no show
  To move, but doth, if the other do.

And though it in the center sit,
  Yet when the other far doth roam,
It leans and hearkens after it,
  And grows erect, as that comes home.

Such wilt thou be to me, who must,
  Like th' other foot, obliquely run;
Thy firmness makes my circle just,
  And makes me end where I begun.

JOHN KEATS

On First Looking into Chapman's Homer

Much have I travell'd in the realms of gold,
  And many goodly states and kingdoms seen;
  Round many western islands have I been
Which bards in fealty to Apollo hold.
Oft of one wide expanse had I been told
  That deep-brow'd Homer ruled as his demesne;
  Yet did I never breathe its pure serene
Till I heard Chapman speak out loud and bold:
Then felt I like some watcher of the skies
  When a new planet swims into his ken;
Or like stout Cortez when with eagle eyes
  He star'd at the Pacific—and all his men
Look'd at each other with a wild surmise—
  Silent, upon a peak in Darien.

Thank You

First and foremost, thanks to all members of the original 52 online group – including those we called 'lurkers'. Like Scheherazade, I kept posting because I knew that there was an appetite for the next episode – and also that I might be killed if it was not delivered on time.

Particular thanks to Norman Hadley, beloved Head Boy and second-in-command at 52. His support, energy and immensely generous gift of time made it possible to keep 52 going when its scale and activity threatened to overwhelm me.

Thanks, of course, to the crowd-funders who made it possible to produce this book and its predecessor, an anthology of poems from members of the online group. Without them, the expensive business of seeking permission to reproduce the poems in this book would not have been possible.

Thanks to the ten guest poets who each wrote a wonderful post for the 52 blog, and to Jade Cancelliere who did a fantastic job of tracking down the permissions from publishers all over the world, negotiating fees and getting the information to me on time.

Jane Commane at Nine Arches Press continues to be an exemplar of patience, dedication to poetry and damn hard work; it is, as always, a great pleasure to put out a book with the Nine Arches emblem on its cover.

Many thanks are due to the following people, who generously crowdfunded this anthology and made its publication possible:

Rob Miles, David C Byrne, Robert Peett, Charlotte Ansell, Steve Harrison, Nina Lewis, Seni Senivaratne, Petra Vergunst, Amali Rodrigo, John Lanyon, Cath Blackfeather, June Palmer, Barbara Marsh, Andy Jackson, Neil Fawcett, Claire Trevien, Matthew Dunford, Elaine Taylor, Lesley Ingram, Martin Shone, Tom Sastry, Sarah Walsh, Ina Anderson, Denni Turp, Tony Walsh, Simon Williams, Eric Bones, Clive Dee, Scott Edward Anderson, Sue Millard, Andrew Bailey, Judith Taylor, Gary Carr, Fran Baillie, Steve Smart, Sharon Black, Colin Davies, Mark Hutchinson, David Clarke, Robbie Burton, Christine York, Stella Wulf, Emma Purshouse, Nicholas Whitehead, AF Harrold, Sarah Bryson, Jane Baston, Carolyn O'Connell, Eilidh Thomas, Gillian Mellor, Kate Bendelow, David Lukens, Rachel Mann, Sue Kindon, Helen Clare, Mandy Pannett, Marc Woodward, John Mackie, Peter Raynard, Abegail Morley, Sallie Tams, Julia Webb, Miki Byrne, Charlie Jordan, Emma Simon, Mandy McDonald, Anne Marie Dagostino, Ailsa Holland, Alwyn Marriage, Char March, David Nicholson, Knotbrook Taylor, Sue Barnard, Naomi Crosby, Elaine Christie, Myfanwy Fox, Bernard Briggs, Shirley Wright, Sarah L Dixon, David Mack, Mavis Moog, Christo Heyworth, Dorothy Baird, Jeff Price, Stephanie Arsoska, Janice Windle, Marily Francis, Meg Cox, Lucy Jeynes, Matthew West, Kate Feld, Hannah Linden, Ben Banyard, Haworth Hodgkinson, Babs Knightley Short, Fiona Russell Dodwell, Marilyn Hammick, Nicky Phillips, Bare Fiction, Max Wallis,

Maureen Cullen, Kathryn Whitehead, Daniel Hooks, Jenny Hill, Julie Bird, Renita Boyle, Kate Fox, Tania Hershman, Ann Follows, Ruth Stacey, Bob Hill, Sharon Larkin, Sandra Gordon, Kevin Reid, Sally Evans, Becky Gethin, Hilary Robinson, Faye Godfrey, Roz Goddard, Carole Bromley, Nina Simon, Jessica Wortley, Trish Traynor, Dru Marland, Mildred Beere, Sarah Watkinson, Julian Dobson, Rayya Ghul, Kymm Coveney, Chris Hemingway, Lindsay Waller Wilkinson, Beth McDonough, Clare Hepworth Wain, Gram Joel Davies, Jackie Biggs, Holly Magill, Brett Evans, Angela Readman, William Gallagher, Jean Atkin, Sarah Maitland Parks, Lesley Quayle, Helen Cadbury, Maggie Mackay, Liz Williamson, Kathy Gee, Jennifer Taylor, Nell Nelson, Bernie Cullen, John and Liz Mills, Michael Mackian, Selkirk Ayres, John Michael Alwyine-Mosely, Tom Freshwater, Reuben Woolley, Mary Gilonne, Rachael Clyne, Josephine Corcoran, Roisin Bourne Hill, Ruth Aylett, Zelda Chappell, Jane Burn, Natalie Baron, Lindsay MacGregor, Angi Holden, Norman Hadley, Susan Castillo, Marjorie Nielson, Liz England, Clare Bold, Jinny Fisher, Judi Sutherland, Raine Voss, Colin Will, Cathy Dreyer, Frances Passmore, Lesley Reid, Phil Ward, Fran Wilde, Mark Gamble, Kriss Nichol, Pauline Sewards, C Edwards, Julie Sorrell, Joanne Key, Jayne Stanton, Sue Sims, Arwen Webb, Big Mamma Frog, Michael Brewer, Jamie Summerfield, Peter Doyle, Peter Richards, Jessica Davies, Margaret Walker, Martin Whatmuff, Brenda Read-Brown, JA Mcgowan, GH Turner.

Acknowledgements

We are grateful to the following publishers, poets and copyright holders who have kindly granted permission for the the poems that appear in this book.

7301 by U.A. Fanthorpe – Reprinted by permission of RV Bailey.

Abebe, the cook's son! by Chris Beckett. From *Ethiopia Boy* (2013, Carcanet) reprinted by permission of Carcanet Press Limited.

After a Greek Proverb by A.E. Stallings – From *Poetry* magazine, Jan 2012. Reprinted by permission of the author.

Against Naturism by Roddy Lumsden – From *Mischief Night: New and Selected Poems* (Bloodaxe Books 2004). Reprinted by permission of Bloodaxe Books Ltd, www.bloodaxebooks.com.

Anne Hathaway by Carol Ann Duffy – From *The World's Wife* (Picador: reprints edition, 2010) Reprinted by permission of Macmillan Publishers Limited.

At the Galleria Shopping Mall by Tony Hoagland – by permission of the author. Taken from Tony Hoagland's forthcoming collection *Application for Release from the Dream* (Bloodaxe Books, 2015). Tony Hoagland is one of America's foremost poets: a good selection of his work can be seen at poetryfoundation.org. He is published in the UK by Bloodaxe Books.

Barracks Snorers by Josh Ekroy – From *Ways to Build a Roadblock*, Nine Arches Press, 2014. Reprinted by kind permission of the author and Nine Arches Press.

Fishing the Balvaig by Norman MacCaig – From *The Poems of Norman MacCaig* (Birlinn, 2011). Reprinted by permission of Birlinn Limited.

Gerald Variations by Luke Kennard – Reprinted by permission of the author.

Gift by Peter Carpenter – From *After the Goldrush*, Nine Arches Press, 2009. Reprinted by kind permission of the author and Nine Arches Press.

Going Home: New Orleans by Sheryl St. Germain – From *Let It Be a Dark Roux: New and Selected Poems.* Copyright © 2007 by Sheryl St. Germain. Reprinted with the permission of The Permissions Company, Inc., on behalf of Autumn House Press, www.autumnhouse.org.

Heritage by Claire Crowther – From *Mollicle*, Nine Arches Press, 2010. Reprinted by kind permission of the author and Nine Arches Press.

If In America by Ed Bok Lee – From *Whorled*. Copyright © 2011 by Ed Bok Lee. Reprinted with the permission of The Permissions Company, Inc. on behalf of Coffee House Press, www.coffeehousepress.com.

in dreams by Daniel Sluman – From *the terrible*, Nine Arches Press, 2015. Reprinted by kind permission of the author and Nine Arches Press.

Keith Standing by Peter Carpenter – From *After the Goldrush*, Nine Arches Press, 2009. Reprinted by kind permission of the author and Nine Arches Press.

Landscape and I by Norman MacCaig – From *The Poems of Norman MacCaig* (Birlinn, 2011). Reprinted by permission of Birlinn Limited.

Large Intestine by Anna Swir – From *Talking to My Body*, translated by Czeslaw Milosz and Leonard Nathan. Copyright © 1996 by Czeslaw Milosz and Leonard Nathan. Reprinted with the permission of The Permissions Company, Inc. on behalf of Copper Canyon Press, www.coppercanyonpress.org.

Lifted by Jo Bell – From *Kith*, Nine Arches Press, 2015. Reprinted by kind permission of the author and Nine Arches Press.

Like the Blowing of Birds' Eggs by Neil Rollinson – Reprinted by permission of the author.

"Look here Vita" quote from Virginia Woolf – Random House, Thomas Atkins.

Lowedges by Helen Mort – From *Division Street*, (Chatto & Windus 2013). By permission of Penguin Random House UK.

Macaronic (L'exilé qui a perdu sa langue…) by Philip Gross – Reprinted by permission of the author.

Machines by Michael Donaghy – From *Dances Learned Last Night: Poems 1975-1995*, (Picador 2000). Reprinted by permission of Macmillan Publishers Limited.

Man in Space by Billy Collins – From *The Art of Drowning*. Copyright © 1995 by Billy Collins. All rights are controlled by the University of Pittsburgh Press.

Oatmeal by Galway Kinnell – From Selected Poems (Bloodaxe Books, 2001). Reprinted by permission of Bloodaxe Books Ltd, www.bloodaxebooks.com.

Pathology of Colours by Dannie Abse – From *New and Collected Poems* (Hutchinson, 2003). By permission of Penguin Random House UK.

Piggotts by Martin Figura – by permission of the author and Arrowhead Press. Originally published in Whistle (2010, Arrowhead Press).

Preston North End by George Szirtes – from *New & Collected Poems* (Bloodaxe Books, 2008). Reprinted by permission of Bloodaxe Books Ltd, www.bloodaxebooks.com.

Raz el Hanout by Rhoda Janzen – by permission of the author. First published in *Poetry* magazine, 2009.

Refrigerator, 1957 by Thomas Lux – From *Selected Poems 1982-2012* (Bloodaxe Books, 2014). Reprinted by permission of Bloodaxe Books Ltd, www.bloodaxebooks.com.

Rising Damp by U.A. Fanthorpe – Reprinted by permission of RV Bailey.

Singh Song! by Daljit Nagra – From *Look We Have Coming to Dover!* (Faber & Faber, 2007). Reprinted by permission of Faber & Faber Ltd.

Taking a Headbutt by William Letford – From *Bevel* (Carcanet, 2012) reprinted by permission of Carcanet Press Limited.

The Afterlife: Letter to Sam Hamill by Hayden Carruth – from *Doctor Jazz*. Originally in *Poetry* (January 1999). Copyright © 1999, 2001 by Hayden Carruth. Reprinted with the permission of The Permissions Company, Inc. on behalf of Copper Canyon Press, www.coppercanyonpress.org

The Door by Charles Tomlinson – From *Selected Poems* (Carcanet, 1999) reprinted by permission of Carcanet Press Limited.

The Race by Sharon Olds – From *The Father* (Cape, 2009) By permission of Penguin Random House UK.

The Way We Live by Kathleen Jamie – From *Mr & Mrs Scotland are Dead: Poems 1980-1994* (Bloodaxe Books, 2002). Reprinted by permission of Bloodaxe Books Ltd, www. bloodaxebooks.com.

Three by David Morley – from *The Night of the Day*, Nine Arches Press, 2009. Reprinted by kind permission of the author and Nine Arches Press.

To Judgment: An Assay by Jane Hirshfield – From *After* (Bloodaxe Books, 2006). Reprinted by permission of Bloodaxe Books Ltd, www.bloodaxebooks.com.

Unsung by Kei Miller – From *A Light Song of Light* (2010, Carcanet) reprinted by permission of Carcanet Press Limited.

Watching for Dolphins by David Constantine – From *Collected Poems* (Bloodaxe Books, 2004). Reprinted by permission of Bloodaxe Books Ltd, www.bloodaxebooks. com.

"What Do Women Want?" by Kim Addonizio –From *Tell Me*. Copyright © 2000 Kim Addonizio. Reprinted with the permission of The Permissions Company, Inc., on behalf of BOA Editions, Ltd., www.boaeditions.org.

Wind by Ted Hughes – From *Collected Poems* (Faber & Faber, 2005). Reprinted by permission of Faber & Faber Ltd.

Where poems are not mentioned in the acknowldegements, they are in the public domain.